GENEALOGICAL RESEARCH GUIDE TO GERMANY

By
Margaret Krug Palen

HERITAGE BOOKS, INC.

Published 1988 By

HERITAGE BOOKS, INC.
1540E Pointer Ridge Place, Bowie, Maryland 20716
(301)-390-7709

ISBN 1-55613-122-4

TABLE OF CONTENTS

ACKNOWLEDGEMENTS

Permission to reproduce Plates 33, 34, 36, and 38 was granted by RVG Rheingauer Verlagsgesellschaft m.b.H., Eltville am Rhein, West Germany.

Permission to reproduce the map on page 40 was granted by Ravenstein Verlag GMBH Bad Soden/Taunus, West Germany.

Permission to reproduce the maps on pages 34 and 35 was granted by Everton Publishers, Inc. Maps originally appeared in *The Atlantic Bridge To Germany Volume II* by Charles M. Hall.

PREFACE

Grandma Krug's death during the worst of the Great Depression left Grandpa Krug to live part of each year with his four sons and their families on the four farms owned by Grandpa - an extended family farming operation. I have childhood memories of mealtime table conversations with Grandpa Krug, when he told about his parents' and grandparents' home in Germany. These conversations - the only time Grandpa spoke in English, his second language - were the beginning of my interest to search my ancestry in the Old World.

Grandpa Henry John Krug was born on 9 February 1872, almost a year after his father, John Peter Krug, had taken an oath of intention to become a citizen of the United States and a little over a year before naturalization on 4 March 1873. Like his father, Grandpa loved to talk about Germany - the birthplace of his parents and grandparents. Two generations emigrated together to the United States in 1865.

Father, Walter William August Krug, the second bilingual generation born in America, was a talking book of family history. He learned family history playing the traditional German culture birthday game at extended family reunions each summer, at German wedding receptions, and at Second Christmas Day gatherings. But Father was not interested in tracing his family in their native village in Germany. He had vivid memories of his German-born relatives that were sacred, but Americanization was his greatest interest and concern during his lifetime. Two wars with Germany in the Twentieth Century made him further disinterested in the Old World. "The German language will never help you during your lifetime," Father insisted while making sure that his children spoke only English even though he preferred German, his first language, when conversing with his family.

My German ancestors lived in rural central Germany, in the state of Hesse (Hessen in German) in the center of the German Federal Republic (West Germany), where farmland is laid out in strips of grain, hay, and clover. Houses with barns on the ground floor are grouped together with farmland on each side and the Black Forest skirts the edge of the village. I remember Grandpa Krug speaking in English about how his father and grandfather moved from the center of Germany where they lived between two great rivers (the Rhine and the Danube) to the center of the United States where they settled between two great rivers (the Mississippi and the Missouri).

My forefathers sailed from Bremerhaven, Germany, in 1865, took six weeks to cross the ocean, and arrived in New York just as the Civil War was ending. They rode the train from New York to Iowa with soldiers from the Iowa regiment who climbed aboard the train coaches right off the battlefields in their eagerness to return to their native state as hostilities ceased. Tales of the appearance of the soldiers right off the battlefields were often told to me as a child by Grandpa Krug and by my great-uncles who learned them first hand from Great-grandfather John Krug. Great-uncle George Krug repeated them to me as his bon voyage send-off when I departed for Germany, the first family member to return to the "homeland."

Upon arrival from Germany the families of my ancestors settled near each other, living within a two mile radius on the Great Plains prairie.

I dreamed of seeing, in person, the villages of my forefathers but knowledge of the villages' exact locations went to the grave with Great-grandfather Krug in 1926, years before my birth. Whenever I asked, "Where is Lohlbach?", the answer was always, "I don't know." I searched every map of Germany I could find in libraries without success during my years of elementary, high school, and college education.

Memories and hearsay were the only clues to my family's past. I devoted ten years of time to research that eventually led to my first visit to Lohlbach, West Germany. The reward was a homecoming experience in an Old World village that dates back to 800 A.D. I was the first descendant of the Krug, Paar, Moller, Happel, and Michel families to return to Lohlbach since my ancestors' immigration to the United States. I participated in village church homecoming worship services in Lohlbach and Battenhausen, and a reception was held in my honor at the Paul Gerhardt House in Lohlbach. I learned that my ancestors undoubtedly walked from Lohlbach, through Frankenau, to the jurisdiction of Vohl in Hessen-Dornstadt which was considered "foreign soil" in the Old World to gain freedom from the struggle against the oppression of poverty, before continuing on to a New World life in Abraham Lincoln's "the last, best hope of man on earth".

I am especially grateful to my husband who uncomplainingly accompanied me on my travels, driving a car in Europe even though he could not speak, read, or understand a word of German. He also read this manuscript and made suggestions to add to its clarity. My gratitude also goes to Ursula Schonborn of Wesel, West Germany, my devoted friend, interpreter and language translator.

I have written this book to provide impetus to further efforts in searching genealogy in Old World villages, and to promote research of American families of German descent. It is my hope that readers will find excitement and adventure in learning to trace their ancestors and discovering the part those ancestors had in shaping the history of the world. If this book proves to be useful as a basis for a satisfying experience in genealogical research and teaches the reader how to efficiently evaluate the findings of his or her family heritage, it will have served its purpose well.

Margaret Krug Palen

INTRODUCTION

Compared to other cultures of the world, we Americans have a small amount of genealogical history to research: only about two hundred years' worth. The ancient Egyptians, Romans, and Chinese all used histories of families to compile dynastic and local histories, and at times incorporated them into literary works.

People search family history for various reasons. For some it is self-discovery --- the more we know about our ancestors, the more we know about ourselves. A genealogical search is more than just a study of old records: one needs tact and diplomacy to get the cooperation of relatives, librarians, and other potentially helpful people; a new appreciation of history and geography is gained in the research process; early lifestyles of ancestors challenges one's understanding of that time period's economics; you discover that an individual is the product of many ancestors and that the strength of family life is found in knowing who you are.

There are no quick methods of tracing your family history. It takes time to organize genealogical research and hours of talk and/or correspondance with living family members - young and old - to find clues to missing information. The easiest years to collect ethnic genealogical information on immigrants are when the immigrants are still alive; these family members can relate the year of their arrival in the country, the port of entry, mode of transportation from the Old World to the New World, and all the names of relatives they knew in both the Old and New Worlds. Additionally, long lives make it possible to tell about births and deaths of children, grandchildren, and great-grandchildren from memory.

In the ethnic community and German culture of my birth, family tradition decreed a game that was fun, intriguing, and challenging: the Birthday Memory Game. The youngest generation of the family played the game each year on Second Christmas Day, December 26, the traditional extended-family reunion.

While the women gathered in the kitchen to prepare and serve the holiday meal and the men gathered in the living room to join in farming talk, the children found an empty spot in the house to gather in a circle to play the Birthday Memory Game. The object of the game was to see who could correctly recite from memory all the full names (first, middle, and last) and birthdays of the first cousins in the family in proper birth order. It was a game all cousins could participate in. No properties were required to play and the oftener the game was played the easier it became. Usually, one of the older children volunteered to be first to recite. When memory failed the child left the circle. We soon learned to stand in correct birth order thus making it necessary only to concentrate on names, months, days, and years!

There was memory reinforcement through repetition and also through the help of a volunteer uncle, the recognized family genealogy expert, who listened in on the children's playing to see if they were following the rules and reciting correct dates. His expertise in the game developed at a young age when he had played the very same game with the first cousins of his generation.

The Birthday Memory Game developed age sets rapidly, particularly in my father's generation when there were one hundred first cousins (counting both the maternal and paternal sides of the family). Cousins born about the same year often developed lifelong friendships with each other while standing together many times reciting in the Birthday Memory Game. Knowledge gained about relatives in the game frequently was remembered through an entire lifetime. Father needed a pencil and paper in his older years, also a day of time and he could list correctly the names and birth order of all one hundred of his first cousins living and dead.

It is important to be thorough in all genealogy research. For instance, there may be two or more villages of the same name in Europe, but located geographically in completely different areas. That is why it is important to locate the state of residence in the Old Country before finding the village. Religion and geography are also associated in Germany. A Catholic ancestor is most likely to be from southern Germany while an ancestor from northern Germany is most likely to be Lutheran. (There are exceptions, however, and some areas in northern Germany predominate in Catholics, and Lutherans predominate in some areas of southern Germany.)

In tracing your ancestors, you will be traveling "backwards" in time following in the footsteps of each preceding generation. The steps you take in tracing your ancestors may not seem very significant at the time; however, they may lead you to stand on the same soil that nurtured your forebearers.

Though there are variations in records to be found throughout Germany, depending upon location and the existence of civil and/or church recordings from one area of Germany to another, there are certain references, problems and procedures to follow in village research in Germany. The purpose of this book is to describe what one must know and do in German village research regardless of whether one is beginning or advanced in genealogy work.

CHAPTER ONE

History of Germany and Immigration to the United States

A Brief History of Germany

Germany's "First Reich" started with the coronation of Charlemagne in 800 A.D.

By the Sixteenth Century, there was a great religious upheaval going on in the German states. This upheaval began in 1517 when Martin Luther posted his Ninety-Five Theses on the door of the Castle Church in Wittenburg, inaugurating the Protestant Reformation. Religious strife followed, culminating in wars which involved most of Europe. Catholics and Protestants fought each other. Lutheran and Reformed Protestants struggled against each other as well as against the non-conformists. Jews were persecuted. The population was reduced by one-third and life became a struggle for survival in most of Germany.

The struggle for freedom erupted again in 1618 and lasted for thirty years; the struggle was known as The Thirty Years War and it resulted in the destruction of German lands and German people. During the wars of the Seventeenth Century, Prussia, a militarist state, expanded until its growth was temporarily checked by the Napoleonic Wars (1792-1814) which swept Europe and destroyed the Holy Roman Empire. (Both Austria and Prussia were defeated by the French.)

Until 1803, the Holy Roman Empire consisted of about three hundred semi-independent principalities; about one-third were ecclesiastic territories. The last Holy Roman Emperor, Francis II, abdicated on 6 August 1806 and the old Empire came to its end.

The defeat of Napoleon resulted in the formation of the German Confederation in 1815; it was known as the "Second Reich". All ecclesiastic territories were dissolved and spiritual princes abdicated and gave their territories to "temporal princes".

The Austro-Prussian War of 1866 led to the dissolution of the German Confederation.

By 1871, the German Empire was formed under the Prussian leadership of Bismark and Kaiser Wilhelm I, welding separate states together into a unified country which quickly began to experience industrial power and expansion of its territories. Prussian power reached its height under Otto von Bismark, the Iron Chancelor.

World War I (1914-1918) ended the "Second Reich". In 1925, Field Marshal Paul Von Hindenberg was elected to presidency of Weimar Republic.

In 1933, Adolf Hitler was appointed Chancellor by Von Hindenberg, starting Germany's "Third Reich". Adolph Hitler's "Third Reich" brought the various titles and monarchs of Germany into a single union. World War II (1939-1945) ended the "Third Reich." After the end of the Second World War, Germany was divided through the center of the country from north to south. Since 1945, West Germany and East Germany have developed differently in their political institutions, their economic, social and cultural life, and their standards of living. The Brandenburg Gate in Berlin, East Germany, marks the border between East and West Berlin, a divided city with two mayors, two separate currencies, and two distinctively different outlooks on the world.

West Germany is known as the Federal Republic of Germany; it is a federation of states created in 1949 out of Hitler's "Third Reich" and has been occupied since World War II by the United States, Great Britain, and France. The West German states follow the historic lines consolidated after the Napoleonic Wars and the establishment of the "Second Reich" in 1871.

After the Potsdam Agreement of World War II, Russia claimed northeast Prussia, an area which would later be known as East Germany. Parts of eastern Germany, before the division of the land into East and West Germany, were controlled by Poland. Britain, France, the United States, and Russia each had a particular zone of occupation for the rest of what was once all Germany. Berlin was occupied by all four powers. In 1949, a Communist-prepared constitution was adopted in the Russian Zone known as the Deutsches Demokratische Republik (D.D.R.) or the German Democratic Republic (G.D.R.) with East Berlin as its capitol. East Germany has been occupied by Russia since World War II.

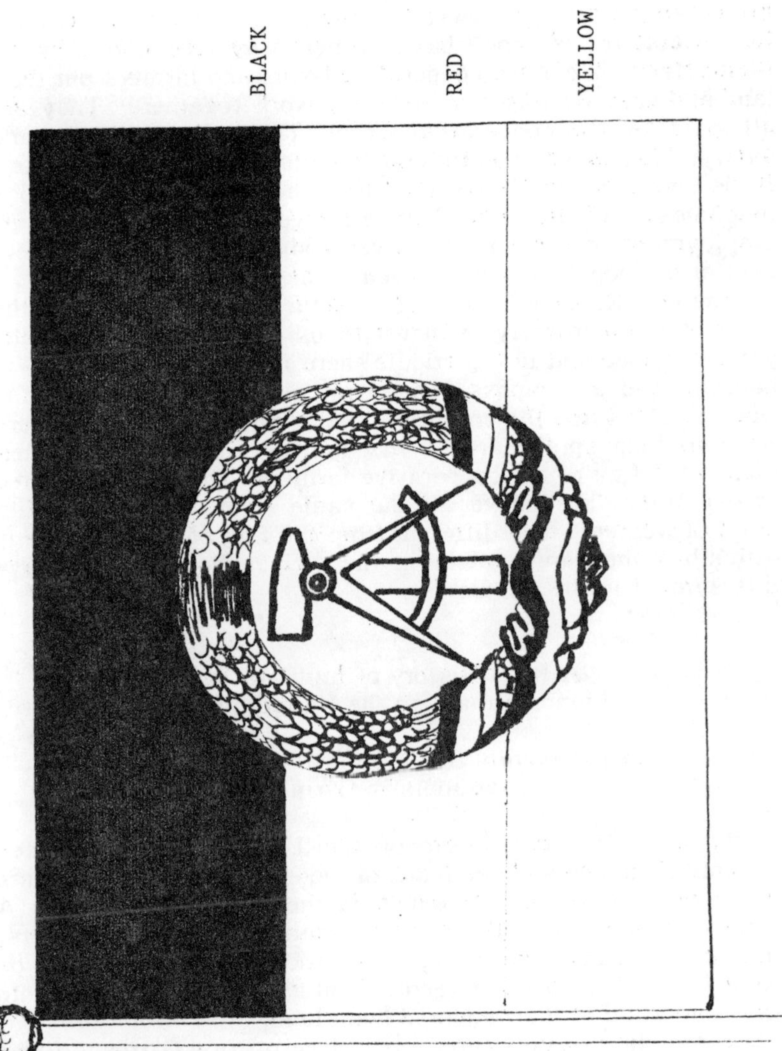

The East German Flag

Our G.D.R. national travel guide, speaking in broken English, explained, "October 5, 1949, the socialist state was founded. That means all things - the schools, all factories, all hotels, etc. - are owned by the state. Also it is the same for agriculture. We don't have farmers anymore who work for themselves. We have cooperative farms and farmers put their land and animals together and they work together. They are all paid by the cooperative farms. They all have the same salary. That is why you find such large fields in our country. It is possible to bring the big machines, the expensive machines, and they use them all together. We have no unemployment in our country. Everybody works. Fifty-five percent of our population are women. They all work."

The G.D.R. guide also explained their national flag, for the most part completely unknown to us. "It is red, black, and yellow striped and in the middle there is a special symbol - a hammer and a compass. That symbol of the hammer is the working class and the compass is the intelligence, and there is something spread around the symbol. It is wheat - that means the flag of the cooperative farmers. They are all united in our state. They have all the same rights in our socialist state of workers. It is different from the flag of West Germany which has the same colors in the stripes but does not have this symbol in the middle."

A Brief History of Immigration from Germany to the United States

Approximately fifty-two million Americans have roots in Germany

By the 1776 birth year of the United States, between seventy thousand and one hundred thousand German emigrants had already taken up residence in the American colonies. A total of two hundred thousand German emigrants - farmers, tradesmen, craftsmen, clergymen, and teachers - settled on American soil in the Eighteenth Century and assimilated into the population of their adopted homeland.

In the Nineteenth Century, over five million Germans found homes in the United States. German emigrants to America surpassed all other emigrant nationalities between the years 1850 and 1885.

Prior to the mid-Nineteenth Century, the basic motives of the craftsmen and small farmers from German states who sailed across the ocean to the New World were primarily economic - at home they were often impoverished and subject to crop failures of cereal grains of rye, oats, and barley, and of potatoes (the mainstay for the lower class people after its introduction into Europe in 1850). Following the Napoleonic Wars, a series of wars took place between France and a number of European nations from 1799 until 1815; the first political refugees from Germany landed in the United States as a result. After the German revolution of 1848, a second wave of political refugees, many from educated classes who embraced the American ideals of civil rights and liberty, immigrated to the United States.

The number of emigrants from Germany increased to over one hundred thousand persons per year in the early to mid-1860's. The emigrants moved west with the great masses of other adventurers and settlers to lands beyond the Mississippi River in a developing United States.

An important influence of German immigrants on the American way of life was their clinging to the concept of the "continental Sunday", a day of churchgoing, picnics, and visiting; it was the only day in the week to relax from labors and carry on the age-old traditions of the fatherland. Many German-American names - Guggenheim, Steinway, Strauss, and Heinz, to name a few - were connected with America's rise to economic power following the Civil War years.

New German immigrants brought with them their national foods, prejudices, and customs; their cultural heritage was reflected in their values, goals, and religious beliefs. But upon arrival in the United States, the American assimilation process changed their language, educated their children, and influenced the running of their businesses. When the First World War began, second generation German-Americans were already so assimilated that only their names were an indication of their German ancestry. However, the outbreak of the First World War rekindled anti-German feelings toward anyone with German thoughts or even a German name.

After Hitler declared war on the United States in 1941, a second wave (the first wave was during World War I) of anti-German feelings in the Twentieth Century swept the American nation. President Truman stated that the United States had fought not against Germany but against Hitler, making a distinction too fine for many Americans to understand. Then in May 1945, a team of German rocket scientists with their director, space travel pioneer Werhner von Braun, were interned by Americans and later flown to the United States to become naturalized citizens in the aftermath of World War II. The advanced technical knowledge of the German scientist was respected and sought after for the advancement of the American culture and way of life. It was a positive step in attitude towards Germany and the Germanic people.

Despite the fact that Germany was the first European nation to develop the scientific aspect of genealogy, the two wars with Germany in the Twentieth Century discouraged German-Americans from openly identifying their origin.

Declining Interest in German Ancestry

"Don't ever mention the word German or that you are German," Father scolded my sisters and I when World War II broke out with Germany in 1942. Non-related neighbors and friends became hostile and suspicious toward anything labeled German when the United States was at war with Germany. The German culture of my family and relatives suffered oppression during the war years because family members had maintained German traditions and values.

International themes grew increasingly popular after the creation of the United Nations following World War II. National pride in the form of native costumes, folk dances, and crafts of many European cultures were displayed. No one, however, mentioned the German culture or attempted to know anything about the ethnic German heritage. Recent educational evaluations have shown that there has been a serious erosion of interest in and commitment to the study of the German language in the United States.

In the summer of 1982, a West German made a small, anonymous gift to the Iowa State University. It was his wish that this gesture should serve as a seed from which long-term efforts to expand German-American relations should grow. A charitable, tax-deductible fund - called the German Project Fund - was established within the Iowa State University Achievement Foundation. Accomplishments and activities of the fund included the 1983 celebration of three hundred years of German immigration to North America. This was an early attempt to raise interest in the German culture and to make known the significant contributions to America's cultural heritage which have been made by generations of German immigrants in Iowa.

First- and second-generation German-Americans had been primarily interested in integration and Americanization. Third- and fourth-generation German-Americans are becoming ethnic conscious and are showing an interest in tracing their German family history back to its European origins.

A Brief History of Life in Löhlbach & Hessen, Germany, in the 1860's to 1880's

In the 1860's in Löhlbach, the living room was used also as a bedroom and four-poster, curtained beds were in common use. Married couples slept together in a straw-sack bed. Very often two, three, or even four children had to share one bed. Other common pieces of furniture included a carved cradle, table with lathe turned curve-shaped legs, wooden chairs with carved back-rests, a spinning-wheel (which was worked on nearly all day long by the grandmother, an unmarried aunt in the house, the mother, or a girl aged twelve or older), a long bench, windows without mountings (they only could be opened by sliding and had small leaded panes), a grandfather clock (often so big that, as in Grimm's fairytale of the seven little goats, the youngest could hide in it and be safe from the wicked wolf), and a lamp-stand.

A Hessen Farmer's Family
Prior to a Meal of Boiled Potatoes And Milk
(Curtained bed at left)

Floors were not painted. They were swept with birch-wood brooms and, on Sundays, white sand bought at the grocer's was spread on the floor. The scrubbing of the rough floors could not be done frequently because much water and working time was needed. Old people often grumbled and complained at "all that scrubbing" because the floors did not dry before evening. Walls were not papered but were whitewashed and speckled with blue dots applied with flax thread.

Until about 1900, Löhlbach villagers had to fetch their water from the nearby creek or from one of the forty-two wells that existed in the village. Children had half-sized tin pails and had to keep the family's kitchen water barrel always filled. Wash day was a long day of hard work. Washing was done with pot-ash lye, soft soap, grained soap, a washing board and wooden tub; those who lived close to the creek did their washing right in the creek, however, and dispensed with the wooden tub. The cattle were watered at the creek. In winter, the frozen creek had to be hacked open. After a thunder storm, all the water was muddy and except for three wells in the village the water was undrinkable until the silt had settled.

Girl Carrying Loaves Of Bread

Villagers in Löhlbach cooked over an open fire through the late 1800's. Prior to 1880, the kitchens were small and primitively arranged; after 1880, the hearth was kept brightly scrubbed. (Wilhelm Busch represented the former type of kitchen in his rascal stories concerning Max and Moritz (1858) in illustrations which showed a large smoke receptacle over a broad hearth.) Many families, however, then replaced the open hearth with a tile stove; only the stovepipe was directed in from the outside. The oven door was made by the village blacksmith. The village blacksmith lived on Water Street in Löhlbach through the 1880's and made oven doors from stretched out metal wagon wheel rims.

Meat and sausage could not be bought in Löhlbach or at nearby Frankenau until after 1906 when butcher Peter Ludde established the "ZurAulisburg Inn" (Aulis Castle) which included a butcher shop. Before 1906 the villagers raised their own meat in a barn attached to their house. Today, the small ground floor barn pens still house a hog, a sheep, and/or a cow and calf in each household.

Until 1900, clothing worn by Löhlbachers was made from local sources of hand-spun wool and coarse hand-woven linen. Both materials were long-wearing and clothing was handed down from generation to generation when parents cut out children's garments from larger pieces of worn fabric.

Linen was produced from flax grown by every farmer in Löhlbach. It was weeded, pulled up, dried, broken, swung, spun, spooled on "pipes" or beams, and woven into fabric. Linen was made into bed cloth; towels; blue smocks worn by boys and men (as can be seen in old Löhlbach school photographs); shirts, bodices, and aprons; (underwear as it exists today was as yet unknown); large sacks for fruit and potatoes; and smaller sacks for transporting all kinds of goods when villagers walked "across the country" (walking was a favorite pastime and exercise of Löhlbachers). It was a long way and many steps from the flax plant to the woven linen. Today, the tools for this process do not exist in Löhlbach and Löhlbachers do not know how to use such equipment.

Homespun, made from lambswool, was knitted into stockings, undershirts, scarfs, wraps, gloves, cuffs, and nightcaps for old men of the village.

The five tailors of Löhlbach up until 1900, when the first sewing machines appeared in the village, had no tools other than a ruler, scissors, thread, and needle. From linsey-woolsey, a most robust coarse fabric of wool and linen, they tailored skirts for girls and women, and trousers and jackets for men.

Plate 38

Plate 34

In the German state of Hessen, the oldest and simplest costume worn by both sexes was a loose-fitting tunic called the "Saxon Smock" (Fig. A, Plate 34); it is still worn today in some form in many parts of the world.

Costumes for men in Hessen were historically geared to practical use, making them simple and very plain. The Sunday costume for men for many years was a long, dark blue coat which went to the knees, had light blue or white lining, pockets and wide cuffs, and was decorated with rows of yellow metal buttons. Pants (of dark blue cloth) were fastened with four metal buttons and a cloak below the knee. Vests were of a dark blue material lined with rows of metal buttons; the shirt collar turned down over a black silk neckscarf. White or light blue stockings and dark blue wool leggings were worn; black leather shoes with tongues adorned with silver buckles or leather strings covered the feet. For a head covering, men wore broad-brimmed hats of black felt. For work, village men generally dressed in coarse handwoven linen with a lightweight coat called a kittel (it extended to the knees), and a knitted woolen stocking cap. On working days, young men wore a blue linen overshirt and a small round black felt hat.

As clothing changed from the loose-fitting tunic to shirts, skirts, bodices, and fitted vests, Hessen women wore many petticoats, reportedly as many as fourteen layers! Each layer was worn above the other, causing the top one to look shorter. The many layers prevented the skirt of black linsey-woolsey, moderately pleated reaching in length to the calf from falling straight down and also broke falls when folk dancing was fast and sometimes wild (Fig. E, plate 36).

Women's frocks were dark-colored and made of self-trimmed linen cloth or thick wool ("linsey-woolsey") (Fig. D, plate 34) Black was the main color worn by Hessen village women; colorful embroideried trimmings and silk ribbons adorning young girls' clothing gave the costume an effulgent and fresh look (Fig. H, plate 33) After marriage, young matrons continued wearing the same colorful costume until the next death in the family; from then on, the costume was made of more somber colors. The skirt was of black linsey-woolsey, with pleats that hung to the calf of the leg. The shirt was either blue or black (white for a dance) (Fig. E, plate 36), and its sleeves reached down to the elbows. it was common for the women in their homes to wear the shirt with sleeves rolled up to the elbows (Fig. G, plate 33). Women wore a camisole or bodice of dark blue linen over the shirt. It was quite common in Hessen to wear a high bodice of dark cloth, wool or velvet, covering the main part of the back and the sides on the upper part of the body, fastened to the upper part of the under-skirt, closing in front with two rows of buttons or tied by traversing cords to hold a bib called a "chest cloth" made of colorful embroidery or damask linen with colored flowers. The "chest cloth" is held by the apron in front and is pulled over a piece of cardboard trimmed with colored silk ribbon and/or metallic embroidery (Fig. C, plate 38). The apron was made of dark blue linen (Fig. C, plate 38), sometimes striped, and sewn with wide pleats designed to go around to the back. Close to the seams were sewn two squares of metallic embroidery or colorful tinsel; the embroidery was attached to a very stiff piece of cardboard and was only sewn on the apron when there was a festive occasion to attend. The apron of young girls at a dance was white. Over the shoulder, women wore a black or dark-colored wool challis neck scarf folded in a triangle pulled to the front and fastened loosely near the waistline. Colorful print flowers or embroidery bordered the fringed edges.

Women wore their hair combed severely upward and twisted into a black headdress worn on top of the head; a bow was fastened to the back of the headdress and it had long, broad ribbon streamers; traditional black ribbons of watered silk Moiree were fastened under the chin and shaped into a bow (Fig. D, plate 34). Young girls wore their hair combed upwards and it fell back into long braids coiled under a headdress of bright red wool with colorful embroidery and ribbon streamers on each side (Fig. C, plate 38; Fig. G, plate 33).

Women wore their hair in a black quilted silk headcover called an Abendmahlshaube (Fig. D, plate 34) in Lohlbach and surrounding villages. The wearing of the Abendmahlshaube to Sunday Communion represented symbolically the Christian confession (religion) of the female population. A high value was placed on the head covering because this identified which class the women belonged to and was also worn to make them look prettier and more attractive.

Stockings were of white wool with triangle-pattern designs (Fig. E, plate 36); seldom did women have colorful decorations on their stockings. Young women wore garters fastened in place using silk decorated ribbons with red woolen pompoms that hung from the knee and swung with movement of the legs (Fig. C, plate 38). Women and girls wore black leather shoes with tongues decorated with buckles or black leather cut-out shoes decorated with black ribbon rosettes (Fig. H, plate 33). Jewelry consisted of necklaces of amber and glass beads, pearls which closed with a silver clasp, or they wore a black ribbon tie which hung down at the neck.

Plate 36

Plate 33

At weddings, dances, and other festive occasions, young men and boys wore white pants and blue jackets (Fig. F, plate 36). On Sunday and at festivals, young men wore green or red caps made out of velvet and gold cord or tassels decorated with otter fur. A white embroidered shirt collar was worn over a silk necktie decorated with gold and silver embroidery (Fig. F, plate 36). Over the shirt, a vest with a standup collar made of Merino wool was decorated with colorful stitchery, gold and patterned buttons, blue ribbons, and a cord design. Over this vest was worn a second vest which was a little bit longer and of dark blue cloth; the corners and pocket flaps and back were stitched with blue silk in a flower pattern; each side had a row of patterned metal buttons. This overvest was without a collar. A jacket was worn over both vests (Fig. F, plate 36); the jacket was one inch longer than the overvest and had sleeves but material color and pattern was exactly like the blue overvest.

For festive occasions, young men wore white linen or leather trousers which were fastened by ribbons strung through zigzag holes and fastened around the knee (Fig. F, plate 36). The men's stockings were of patterned white embroidered wool. The heavy leather shoes were cobbled from foot to ankle with laces and a buckle.

At festivals the older men had hats of very large size with round, wide brims turned up on three sides and fastened with a button and with black ribbons.

CHAPTER TWO

Research To Do In The United States

The first step is to start with yourself and write down all of the information handed down in your family by word of mouth. How much do you actually know about your family - parents, grandparents, great-grandparents, aunts, uncles, and cousins? Oral traditions are useful as guidelines and as hints leading to further research but are often laced with innocent (and sometimes not so innocent) mistakes; thus, oral tradition must be verified using primary and secondary sources.

Primary sources

These types of records are made by the people involved in the event or occasion; such records provide first-hand evidence and are of greater reliability and credibility than secondary sources. Primary sources include such things as:

birth, marriage, and death certificates - vital in reconstructing family lineage; some communities in the United States did not begin officially recording vital statistics until the beginning of the Twentieth Century; however, there are a number of community records going back to the Nineteenth Century. *Death certificates* often additionally give birth date and place as well as the next of kin (if known), and name of the widow(er), and may be located in city halls or county courthouses; some states have centralized these records in the state capitol. *Birth certificates* give the individual's full name and date and place of birth as well as parents' names. *Marriage certificates* give the name of the married couple plus the date and place of marriage.

church records - evidence of vital statistics of members of Lutheran churches, as well as such denominations as Evangelical, Methodist, Baptist, and Protestant Episcopal, are recorded in church books and are usually available upon request from local congregations. Look for baptismal, confirmation, marriage, membership, and cemetery records which include names of spouses or Godparents, parents, and grandparents.

city directories - general collections of United States city directories and telephone books are to be found in town, city and state, libraries and at the Library of Congress in Washington D.C.

school records - verification of birth dates and full names, parents' signatures may be found in school records.

oaths of intention and naturalization records - see Finding Your Immigrant Ancestor

legal contracts - land ownership, sale of property, signature of husbands and wives

tax bills - location, names of owners, residency evidence, years paid

mortgages - names of owners, evidence of years of residency showing location

passports - verify birthdates, country of birth, citizenship

business licenses - occupation, type of business, location of business, partnership

social security cards - verify legal name after 1936

income tax forms - legal names, residency, names of minor children

wills - legal names of children and closest family members

letters - frequently detail names of family members and relatives and events with dates

diaries - often give insights into the personality of your ancestor that cannot be obtained in any other source; clues to political, social, and religious thinking of your family are often recorded in a diary.

census records - microfilm of Federal censuses for the years 1850, 1860, 1870, and 1880 can be photocopied at a fixed price from the National Archives and is an excellent source of information if the residence of the person sought is known. Now available through the program are federal population census schedules, slave schedules, and Soundex indexes, 1790-1910; Revolutionary War service records and index, and Revolutionary War pension and bounty land warrant application files. The film is now available at a new, low price (prices of each roll of microfilm are subject to change without advance public notice): $3 per roll for up to four rolls, $2.50 each for orders of five to nine rolls, and $2.00 each for ten or more rolls. The rental period has been extended to thirty days. To join the program, write: National Archives, Microfilm Rental Program, P.O. Box 2940, Hyattsville, MD

20784; or call (301)-927-3701 to find out which public library nearest you is participating in the program.

military records - there is little information for determining the country of origin of military personnel prior to the Civil War; after the war, records became more specific as to date of birth and often place of birth. Military pension records are an excellent source of information (birth date and place, names of parents, and residency at time of pension). The National Archives houses military records going back to the Revolutionary War. Souvenirs such as uniform buttons, medals, badges, and patches can point to official lists worth checking.

land deeds - when President Abraham Lincoln signed the Homestead Act in 1862, he made possible purchasing of land inexpensively from the Federal government. Homestead records may help in determining residency in the early years of an immigrant's life. The Land Record Office in the National Archives must have a complete description of the land in order to be of assistance to you. If you do not have a complete description of the land, the Register of Deeds in the local county courthouse is the place to search first.

court records - All kinds of family businesses appears in public records made as the result of hearings. A person appearing before a court must give certain information by way of identificiation. Court records bring out this information about family affairs and property. Don't make the mistake of thinking court records only have data on criminal proceedings. Ancestors in Colonial America who served on a jury, for instance, will be listed in a court record. Any relatives that were clerks of a court, a constable, a sheriff or other court officer are easy to find in court records.

Secondary Sources

These types of records were probably written by people who were not eyewitnesses to the event or occasion; thus, such records are not totally reliable and are most useful when backed up by a primary source. Secondary sources include such things as:

cemetery inscriptions - Inscriptions can document the accuracy of what you have verbally accumulated to date. It is important to note, however, that sometimes dates on tombstones are not accurate; occasionally, the person purchasing the stone has only memory to rely on for date information, and you will discover, memory sometimes fails to be accurate. Often adult emigrants from the Old World brought no vital statistic records with them to the New World so that survivors at the time of the emigrants' deaths had no reference to consult for accuracy of dates reported for funeral services and tombstone engraving. This was the case with two generations of emigrants of my Krug ancestors. My Krug great-great-grandparents did not have tombstones with names and dates on them at their burial in St. Stephens Cemetery near Atkins, Iowa. When my father was elected to the cemetery committee, I accompanied him to search for Krug family grave markers by taking measurements out of the cemetery plot book and actually measuring the recorded distances. We successfully found both graves and probed beneath the grown-over grass to uncover cement markers. I made a crayon rubbing of the engraved inscriptions: "Mother" and "F(ather) Krug" still visible in the cement. The English spelling on the headstones of my great-grandparents John Krug (Johannes Peter Krug) and wife, Cathrine (Anna Kathrina Michel) Krug, 1865 emigrants, illustrates the Americanization process and is the only English written record available giving the birth dates (1844 for John and 1848 for Cathrine) needed to trace genealogy back to the Old World. In the village of Geismar, West Germany, however, I found the birth record for Anna Kathrina Michel stated that she was born in 1847. This meant that my Great-grandmother Krug lived one year longer than her American descendants realized at the time of erection of the tomstone.

Bible verses on old tombstones add to your understanding of your heritage and your ancestors' belief system. Tombstone rubbings of them add to family memorabilia collections. My Happel ancestors' grave markers were resplendent with engraved Bible epitaphs in German, and headstones and footstones with inscriptions in both English and German names; they revealed the importance of relating to following generations the beliefs of their Americanized culture.

obituaries - obituaries for family members born in the Old World may include the name of the deceased's native village in Germany.

family Bible records - almost every American family in the early history of our country owned a Bible. Traditionally, the head of the family recorded the important dates of birth, baptism, marriage, death, and burial for each family member.

oral reports - Start with the elderly members of the family whose memories stretch farthest back. Remember to keep an open mind, getting a second opinion or documentation to support the information received.

newspaper clippings - births, birthday parties, marriages, deaths, stories about relatives.

When looking for primary and secondary sources, look to your family first. Relatives may own family Bibles, letters, pictures, journals, and diaries. Some family members may have kept scrapbooks containing such things as newspaper clippings, tombstone inscriptions, and names and addresses of family members. These home collections could hold information and clues to the sponsors and godparents of children, witnesses of deeds and wills, soldier and military records, wills or unrecorded deeds, school diplomas, old passports, social security cards (after 1936), legder books, samplers and quilts, initialed silverware, luggage tags or labels on old trunks (may tell the year when a family moved), neighbors who settled near family members in the United States (if you cannot locate your ancestor's origin in Germany through research on your own family, you may be able to track neighbors and friends to the family home in Germany because emigrants frequently traveled in groups), business partners, travelling companions, and the maiden names of women marrying into your family. If you discover that a family member has already made a record of the information you are seeking, go directly to that person for assistance in furthering your search. (Needless to say, duplicating research already done is wasted effort but do verify any record or records that you feel are questionable.)

The local county courthouse can provide birth, marriage and death documentation as well as records of naturalization, census returns, civil/criminal court cases, land deeds, wills and claims. The records are usually found under the jurisdiction of Record's Clerk.

If the geographical distances are too great to visit a relative, library, or archive a letter of inquiry is the second best approach to gathering information. Letters should be brief and as concise as possible, explaining the reason for your inquiry and asking specific questions in a logical procession. Generally, the more specific the question, the more specific the answer. (Note that libraries and archives may limit your number of questions per letter, charge fees for research, or simply may not have the personnel to do research so a letter requesting their quidelines for research is a good idea.) Note any discrepancies that may appear in your data when you receive answers from your relatives or library researchers. Such discrepancies may be simple errors and further research can resolve conflict. It is important for you, as the genealogist, to decipher where fiction (oral tradition) ends and facts (primary and secondary sources) begin. Searching for the real facts remains the adventure and challenge of the genealogist.

Family History Chart

When you have gathered enough data to complete a generation, you are ready to construct a work sheet known as a family history chart, family tree, or pedigree (ancestor) chart. ("Pedigree" derives from the Latin *pes* (foot) and *grus* (crane); the lines on early family history charts resembled a crane's foot and so the symbol became synonymous with the study of genealogy.) The pedigree (ancestor) chart will be your most valuable research tool to take with you to a village in Germany when you make your inital visit. When completed, a pedigree (ancestor) chart will tell - at a quick glance - the story of family relationships and its vital statistics for four or more generations. Use full names of individuals when filling in the chart - initials and abbreviations may lead to confusion. Dates should be written as day month year (18 August 1782) and never abbreviate the year ('82) or turn the months into numerals (18/8/1782); again, write the dates fully and clearly to avoid possible confusion.

On the chart you are number one. Every father's number is twice that of his child and every mother's number is her husband's number plus one. In other words, all men have even numbers beside their names and all women have odd numbers.

It is a good idea to start by filling out the family history chart in pencil. Later it will be a permanent record when it is complete and can be finished in ink or typewritten. Data stored in a computer can be easily updated and corrected. Some periodicals that deal with computers and genealogy include: *Computer-Genealogist*, 1984, National Society of Computer-Genealogists, Genealogical Center Library, 2815 Clearview Plaza, Atlanta, GA 30340; *Computers in Genealogy*, 1982, Society of Genealogists, 14 Charterhouse Buildings, London, England; *Genealogical Computer Pioneer*, Posey International, Box 338, Orem, Utah 84057; *Genealogical Computing*, (bi-monthly), Transfer, 5102 Pommeroy Drive, Fairfax, Virginia 22032; The Computer Helper column found in *The Genealogical Helper* (bi-monthly), Everton Publishers Inc., 3223 S. Main Street, Nibley, Utah 84321 - (801)-752-6022.

Your full name   Date and place of birth   Residence   Religious affiliation

(maiden name, if any)

Father's name   Date and place of birth   Mother's name   Date and place of birth

(maiden name)

Education   Date and place of marriage   Spouse's name

YOUR CHILDREN

	Sex	Name	When born where	When married where	Married to	If dead, when and where *buried*
1.						
2.						
3.						
4.						
5.						

FAMILY HISTORY

What do you know about the family surname?

Are there traditional first, middle, or nicknames?

Do you know the name of your immigrant ancestor?

What country did he come from?

When and how did he arrive in this country?

Person No. 1 on this chart is identical to person

No.__________ on chart No.__________

b Date of birth
pb Place of birth
m Date of marriage
d Date of death
pd Place of death

1 Margaret Louaive Krug
b 14 May 1931
pb Fremont Twp. Benton Co. Iowa
m 1November 1957
d
pd

NAME OF HUSBAND OR WIFE
Kenneth Raymond Palen

2 Walter William August Krug (Father of No. 1)
b 2 August 1904
pb Clinton Twp. Linn County Iowa
m 9 September 1925
d 8 October 1985
pd Iowa City, Iowa

3 Enid Muriel Bryner (Mother of No. 1)
b 8 June 1903
pb Eldorado Twp. Benton Co. Iowa
d 17 November 1986
pd Vinton, Iowa

4 Henry John Krug (Father of No. 2)
b 9 February 1872
pb Fremont Twp. Benton Co. Iowa
m 9 March 1898
d 26 December 1955
pd Vinton, Iowa

5 Christina Marie Happel (Mother of No. 2)
b 13 Februery 1877
pb Fremont Twp. Benton Co. Iowa
d 17 March 1934
pd Clinton Twp. Linn Co. Iowa

6 Frank Arthur Bryner (Father of No. 3)
b 13 September 1875
pb Mt. Auburn Benton Co. Iowa
m 1 January 1900
d 28 December 1955
pd Salt Lake City, Utah

7 Inez Vivian Tanner (Mother of No. 3)
b 30 January 1877
pb Eldorado Twp. Benton Co. Iowa
d 3 January 1966
pd Cedar Rapids, Iowa

8 JohannesPeter Krug (Father of No. 4)
b 22 January 1844
pb Löhlbach Kurhessen Hessen-Kassel Germany
m 22 August 1869
d 21 June 1926
pd Fremont Twp. Benton Co. Iowa

9 Anna Katharina Michel (Mother of No. 4)
b 30 September 1847
pb Geismar Kreis Frankenberg Kerrhessen Germany
d 30 May 1918
pd Fremont Twp. Benton Co. Iowa

10 Peter Johann Happel (Father of No. 5)
b 4 March 1851
pb Altenhaina Hessen Germany
m 3 July 1874
d 13 May 1902
pd Eldorado Twp. Benton Co. Iowa

11 Katharina Elisabeth Werning (Mother of No. 5)
b 24 January 1854
pb Dankerode an der Fulda Rothenberg Hessen Nassau Germany
d 13 July 1937
pd Van Horne Benton Co. Iowa

12 James Monroe Bryner (Father of No. 6)
b 22 May 1829
pb Uniontown, Fayette Co. Pa.
m 4 October 1861
d 2 December 1911
pd Canon City, Colorado

13 Sarah Caroline Gorden (Mother of No. 6)
b 4 August 1838
pb Cambridge, Illinois
d 7 October 1907
pd Vinton, Iowa

14 William Allen Tanner (Father of No. 7)
b 24 October 1841
pb Wayne Co. Ohio
m 24 December 1869
d 25 September 1880
pd Norway, Iowa

15 Mary Janette Muirhead (Mother of No. 7)
b 20 September 1852
pb Udina, Kane Co. Illinois
d 1 March 1938
pd Cedar Rapids, Iowa

16 Johann Justus Krug (Father of No. 8) — Continued on chart 2
Löhlbach Germany

17 Katharina Elisabeth Paar (Mother of No. 8) — Continued on chart 2

18 Johann Peter Michel (Father of No. 9) — Continued on chart 4
Geismar Germany

19 AnnaElisabeth Freitag (Mother of No. 9) — Continued on chart 4

20 Andreas Happel (Father of No. 10) — Continued on chart 5
Löhlbach Germany

21 Marie Elisabeth Möller (Mother of No. 10) — Continued on chart 5

22 Johann Adam Werning (Father of No. 11) — Continued on chart 8
Dankerode-an-der Fulda Germany

23 Johana Jeanette Brehm (Mother of No. 11) — Continued on chart 8

24 David L. Bryner (Father of No. 12) — Continued on chart 11
Pennsylvania

25 Sarah Bodkin (Mother of No. 12) — Continued on chart 11

26 William Smith Gorden (Father of No. 13) — Continued on chart 12
Kentucky

27 Anna Wilson (Mother of No. 13) — Continued on chart 12

28 John Luther Tanner (Father of No. 14) — Continued on chart 13
Ohio

29 Isabell Kearns (Mother of No. 14) — Continued on chart 13

30 George Muirhead (Father of No. 15) — Continued on chart 14
Scotland

31 Mary Morrison (Mother of No. 15) — Continued on chart 15

Spelling and Pronunciation of Surnames

Name change problem: Many Germans changed their name upon immigrating to America. If pronunciation of the name was difficult, the name was changed to make it easier to say phonetically, (e.g. Möller was changed to Moeller in my father's family and Michel was changed to Michael).

A difficult name change in my family genealogy search was that of Johann Peter Michel, known to all of his family descendants as "Henry". I expected to find Heinrich in the records in Geismar, West Germany, but instead found his name in the Geismar Kirche (church) records as Johann Peter Michel, the same as inscribed on his tombstone in St. Stephens Cemetery near Atkins, Iowa. Then I learned from German friends that "Henry" is one of the most common nick-names in Germany, when accurate names are not spoken.

Cathrine Michel also changed her name in America by dropping her first name, Anna, and changing the spelling of Kathrina to Katherine or Cathrine, making searching her history more difficult.

The L.D.S. (Church of Jesus Christ of Latter Day Saints) Genealogical Library copies records in Germany onto microfiche and is a place to research surnames and village records to determine avenues of future research procedure. The area of Germany my ancestors are from is recorded under the title of Preussen (Prussia), then Hessen, then Nassau, then the village name. Understanding the geographical changes through German history of the area you are researching aids in finding genealogical listings.

It is important to beware of surnames that are the same but which can mislead you in your research. Do not start your search with someone you discover has a similar surname and try to trace them down the centuries to you. It is almost always impossible to be successful with this approach because there is little liklihood that it really is the same family. Begin your search with you and go backwards in time. Krug is a common German surname and a word in the German language (Krug means masculine gender for pitcher, jug, tankard or public house). There are many Krugs listed in the telephone directories of all major American cities. There were even other Krugs that immigrated to the same county in Iowa at the same time as my relatives but to date no relationship has ever been traced to them. Oral tradition in the Krug family from my father and great-uncles is that the other Krugs are *not* related to my family.

The spelling of a name can change because of a preference for the name to be spelled phonetically and because of the desire to Americanize the name. In my search I found that my ancestors with the surname Moeller in the New World had made the decision to Americanize their name Möller. When I began my search in the Old Country, I soon discovered their surname in Germany was spelled Möller. So as you trace be prepared for changes in names. Don't assume that every person who spells their name the same way as you do is related to you, and, conversely, every person whose name is similar, is a potential, if somewhat distant, relative.

You may find that the pronounciation, as well as the spelling, of the surname has changed. The first and second generations of German-Americans in the New World were so concerned with integration and Americanization that they preferred to have their German name sound American. In my family the pronounciation of Krug was changed from the German rolled "r" sound to an Americanized "u" vowel sound that added "rug" to "K". The difference in the sound of the two names was great indeed and made Father and his brothers and cousins feel more Americanized. They never hesitated to correct anyone about the "right" pronounciation using the "rug" sound.

When listening to family stories from relatives and friends or reading family papers, be sensitive to hearing and seeing a name change. The quicker you discover the difference, the more accurate your genealogical research will become.

Name research: It is very important to be absolutely sure of the correct names of immigrant ancestors. If there is any reason to believe that the spelling of a surname may have changed when the family naturalized in the United States, a thorough investigation of all genealogical primary sources to discover when, where, and why the name was changed is needed. Many times, names were simply misspelled and never corrected even on official documents. Johann became John; Heinrich became Henry; Elisabeth became Elizabeth. Great-great-grandfather Johann Justus Krug dropped the use of his first Christian name when he came to the New World, probably so he would not be confused with his immigrant son Johannes, changing Justus to "Gust" for his first name. No one in the American community in which he lived for fourteen years knew his name was Johann Justus. He was simply called "Gust" Krug. Second generation German-Americans in the family assumed his name must be August when learning by oral tradition that he was called "Gust."

Genealogical work is facilitated by familiarizing oneself with all typical misspellings or pronunciation errors associated with a family name before traveling to the native German village. Great-Grandmother's name was spelled Kathrina, Katherine, and Cathrine on various family documents, church records, and tombstones in the United States. Since it was the same person, I was able to figure out from primary sources that the spelling of the name depended upon who was giving the information at the time of recording. Kathrina was Old Country German, Katherine was considered American, and Cathrine was the modern change to her name with the younger New World generation of the family.

The actual study of the origin of names, their meanings, and various spellings is called onomastics. (See the *New Dictionary of American Family Names* by Elsdon C. Smith for an excellent, general overview which explains the evolution of names from occupations, localities, fathers' name, and personal characteristics.) In Lohlbach, West Germany, all the men among my relatives had Christian first names of Johann. At first it was very confusing to learn that all other masculine family names - August, Henrich, George, Conrad, Karl, William (all popular names of European nobility) - were preceeded by the name Johann.

Religion has been an influencing factor in selection of first names for the last two thousand years. The closest Lutheran cathedral to my ancestral villages in the state of Hessen, Germany, is at Marburg Die Elisabeth Kirche, containing a golden shrine to St. Elisabeth, a repose for her earthly remains. This reverence for St. Elisabeth was a factor in the many Elisabeth names of the women in my ancestoral pedigree. In first generation and second generation German-American families living in the United States, it was common for children to have more than one Christian name given to them by godparents. Most first names used in the United States by German families originated from five languages: Hebrew, Teutonic, Greek, Latin, and Celtic.

In 1545, the Catholic Church made use of Saints' names mandatory for baptism resulting in a common usage of the names John and Mary. At the same time, Protestants often used Hebrew names like Elizabeth, Mary, and John. My German ancestors feminized names with simple endings: e.g., Christina for Christian. In tracing my paternal grandmother's name, I found it recorded as either Christina or Christine, depending again upon whether the recorder was thinking in terms of native Old Country German names or Americanized names. In like manner, Great-aunt Lizzy's name was spelled either Elizabeth or Elisabeth (German language spelling).

My German relatives in America preferred to use more than one Christian name with their four letter surname, following the tradition of German nobility by naming children after baptismal sponsors. Father's baptismal sponsors were his paternal uncle, William Krug, and maternal uncle, August Happel; therefore, Father's name became Walter William August Krug.

Finding the Immigrant Ancestor

Naturalization is the process by which an alien becomes a citizen. The requirement of An Oath of Intention to become naturalized existed in the 19th century and the data required varied from jurisdiction to jurisdiction. I found only the age of the applicant, allegiance, and date of declaration when I searched for the documents of John Krug, Henry Michel, Adam Werning, and Andrew Happel, all great-grandfathers of my Krug family genealogy. Before 1866, declarations also included the date and place of residence in the United States and place of embarkation. After 1866 some forms gave a physical description in addition to place of residence, last foreign address, name of ship and port and date of entry. After the oath was taken, a minimum of two years had to pass before naturalization could take place.

From 1790 to 1795, naturalization residence requirements for free, white aliens was one year in a state and two years in the United States. However, in 1795 a change required a residency of five years in the United States. From 1798 to 1802 a fourteen-year residency in the United States was required and the declaration of intention had to be filed five years prior to naturalization. 1802 laws changed requirements back to one year's residence in a state and five years in the United States with declaration of intention filed three years prior to naturalization. The five-year residency requirement remains to the present day.

Certificates of naturalization before 1906 are scattered throughout the United States in the courts - municipal, district, and Federal - where the naturalization took place; these certificates often give the individual's birthplace, date of entry into the United States, and sometimes the name of the vessel on which the emigrant arrived.

Before the Clerk of the District Court appeared John Krug

a native of Prussia aged Twenty-Seven years, who, being duly sworn upon his oath declares that it is BONA FIDE his intention to become A CITIZEN OF THE UNITED STATES, and to renounce forever all allegiance and fidelity to EVERY PRINCE, POTENTATE, STATE AND SOVEREIGNTY WHATSOEVER, and particularly to the Emperor of Germany of whom he is at present a subject.

Sworn to and subscribed before me this 28" day of February 1871

B R [illegible] Clerk.

John Krug

The United States Immigration and Naturalization Service began in 1906; naturalization papers thereafter give the petitioner's name, address, last address in the country of origin, birthplace, parent's names (including mother's maiden name), port of entry into the United States, and date of entry. Copies of declarations and petitions for naturalization may be obtained by sending for form G-641 from the United States Immigration and Naturalization Service, 425 I Street, N.W., Washington, D.C. 20536, and sending the appropriate fee, $15.00 at present. Form G-641 is used to request verification of age or date of birth, naturalization or citizenship, and genealogical information.

Look for naturalization documents to confirm the presence in the United States of your earliest immigrant ancestor and note his or her place of residence in the Old World. (See John Krug, Prussia, 1871 oath of intent and 1873 naturalization document. Appendix.) It is quicker to verify naturalization if you know the county of residence in the United States for your immigrant ancestor; you can then inquire at that county's courthouse Recorder's Office for the documents. If the county of residence is unknown, your only method of obtaining a naturalization document is from the Bureau of Immigration and Naturalization, 425 I Street, N.W., Washington, D.C. 20336.

If you have difficulty locating an immigrant ancestor whose citizenship would have been prior to 1906, read James C. and Lila Lee Neagles' *Locating Your Immigrant Ancestor* (see Bibliography). That will be quicker and less expensive than writing to the Federal government.

Not all aliens took out the final citizenship/naturalization papers. My Great-Great-Grandfather Werning swore an oath of intent to become a citizen on 24 August 1876, at age 64 years, and died three years later without taking out the final naturalization formalities. I searched for naturalization papers for women ancestors until I dsicovered that until 1922 married females automatically became citizens when their husbands received citizenship. Even though unmarried females could go through the naturalization process, few were naturalized for various reasons.

Other records can help you in your search for information on your emigrant ancestor(s):

Ship Passenger Lists - available on microfilm in the National Archives; microfilm may be borrowed through your local library. Some of these lists are indexed, others are not. Beginning in 1820, ships' masters who docked their vessels at any of the chief ports in the United States were required to prepare a passenger manifest which listed his passengers' names, sex, age, occupation, country of nativity, and destination. The ships passenger list immediately gave a profile of my Krug ancestors Elizbeth age 24; Johann age 21, Henrich age 14, Justus age 59, Anna age 54 in 1865. These manifests are on microfilm at the National Archives in Washington, D.C., and will be copied for a fixed fee of $18.00 presently (subject to change without advance public notice), or rent from L.D.S. library for lesser amount. To obtain a copy, you will need to know the name of the vessel, the port of entry, the approximate date of arrival, and the name of the passenger.

Vital records - see Primary Sources.

City Hall in Germany - write to the city hall of the village your ancestors lived in or to the nearest village and request information that will verify place of birth (see illustration and addresses in Bibliography). In parts of Germany all civil records were destroyed in bombing fires during World War II and only church records can be used to locate ancestor's births.

Solving Genealogical Problems

Proof of birth: Vital records (births, marriages, and deaths) were not kept by many state governments during America's first one hundred years. It is common to discover that the only proof of an ancestor's birth is through home records such as the family Bible, various kinds of diaries, journals, and church records. Church records generally include Christenings (baptisms), confirmations, marriages, and burials. Church records were kept usually by the minister and are considered semi-official records because entries are made at or near the day of the event. You will need to know your ancestor's religion. If you cannot find the person's religion, go to a county history and learn about the religious groups that came into the county and when and where they came from. If this does not give you a clue to your ancestor's religion, correspond with the archivist of the predominant church in that area.

Finding Wife's records: Family records in the early history of the United States very often are complete for men, but often fail to list the wife or list only the given name without the surname. The marriage record is the place to look for the wife's surname because her complete name would be required on the document. A wife is required to sign deeds with her husband; however, land records do not give her surname unless there is a second marriage involved and an agreement is made about real property. If the marriage was in the New World, search the nearest and largest county seat records for a marriage license, usually taken out at the residence of the bride.

How to look for inaccuracies in records: Records filled with generalities and "abouts" should be checked for accuracy. Years ago libraries accepted research without verification so that it is necessary to be alert for inaccuracies in records which cause the researcher to go off in a wrong direction. The lack of a complete locality name can be misleading in genealogical research. Two persons by the same name may have lived in the same locality as was true in the case of my search for the naturalization records of John Krug in Benton County, Iowa. Two John Krugs from the state of Hessen, Germany, were recorded in Benton County in different years as filing on oath of intention to become citizens. Only the age difference recorded descerned which was my ancestor's record. The lack of recording the source of information is a warning of inaccuracy in research. When a source is cited the record has been created from original records and verified so that it will stand forever. It is possible to add new and additional information, but the record will not be subtracted from or basically changed.

Conclusion

Exhaust all possible records available to you in this country that are necessary to find the immigrant ancestor(s) in your family before you travel to the Old World. Having done this, you will then have all the data available State-side with you to confirm or question data you collect in Germany. Check what you have found for the following points:

What do you know about the immigrants ancestor's surname in the Old World?

Do you know where your ancestors came from - not just from Germany, but the exact place in that country?

How did they earn a living?

What were their talents and abilities?

What clothing did they wear?

What was it like living in Germany at the time of immigration?

What motivated them to leave a land and people they loved?

It is fun to discover ancestors. By learning about ancestors, we discover how much their values and goals can teach us even today. The search for your ancestors is not complete, however, without a personal trip to the land from which they came. It takes persistence to have a foreign adventure but the reward is learning many things you cannot find out in any other way.

A foreign vacation is the perfect opportunity for a pilgrimage to your ancestral village. Then you can see ethnic customs first hand, taste native foods, and take part in traditions of your native culture. You become personally involved with local inhabitants of the village and can find a link with the past in the Old Country records. You will have the experience of walking the streets your ancestors walked, visiting the homes in which they lived, and worshiping in the church in which they worshiped.

So the starting point in tracing your ancestry begins with yourself and the oral traditions handed down to you. As you question what information about yourself to record, you'll learn what questions to ask of others in your family search. In the process of recording your own date and place of birth, you will learn to ask questions:

Were you born in a city hospital or was it a rural birth? My birth "on a farm in Fremont township, Benton County, Iowa", is an example of the correct way to record a rural birth.

What is your correct address now? The place of residence is where the person is living at the time you fill out the Family History Chart.

What was your mother's maiden name? In order to be accurate in genealogy research, the maiden surname is needed as well as the first and middle names of the mother or wife.

The answers to these family history questions will reveal any oral traditions that exist. It is important to follow oral tradition answers on every question listed for each family until primary and secondary sources can be researched.

Where is the family cemetery located? Precise directions such as "St. Stephens Cemetery is located one mile west and one mile south of the town of Atkins, Benton County, Iowa," make it possible to locate and visit the cemetery in future research.

It is a good idea to work on one side of your family at a time to prevent confusion of names. If, however, two sides of your family came from the same village or town in Germany, you will save time and money (especially once you are overseas) by working on them simultaneously. In my family search I discovered as I went along that the Krug, Happel,

Paar, and Möller families all lived in the same village of Löhlbach, West Germany, at various times. The Happel family also lived in the nearby village of Altenhaina located in the same parish of the Löhlbach church (Kirche). And the wives of the Happel generations came from the village of Battenhausen, another part of the Löhlbach parish. The proximity of the villages is vividly shown on this Wanderkarte Map (Hiking) used by the many German vacationers visiting the Löhlbach Spa and walking the trails around Lohlback.

North Americans do not understand the complex boundaries of the many villages in Germany and a look at a map of the exact area of interest must be made to fully comprehend the challenge to the researcher of genealogy in Germany. See Frankenberg and Rotenberg inserts.

Frankenberg, State of Hessen, Germany
Showing the village boundaries of Lohlbach, Atlenlotheim, Baltenhausen, and Geismar, home of my Krug, Poar, Hoppel, Möller, and Michel ancestors.

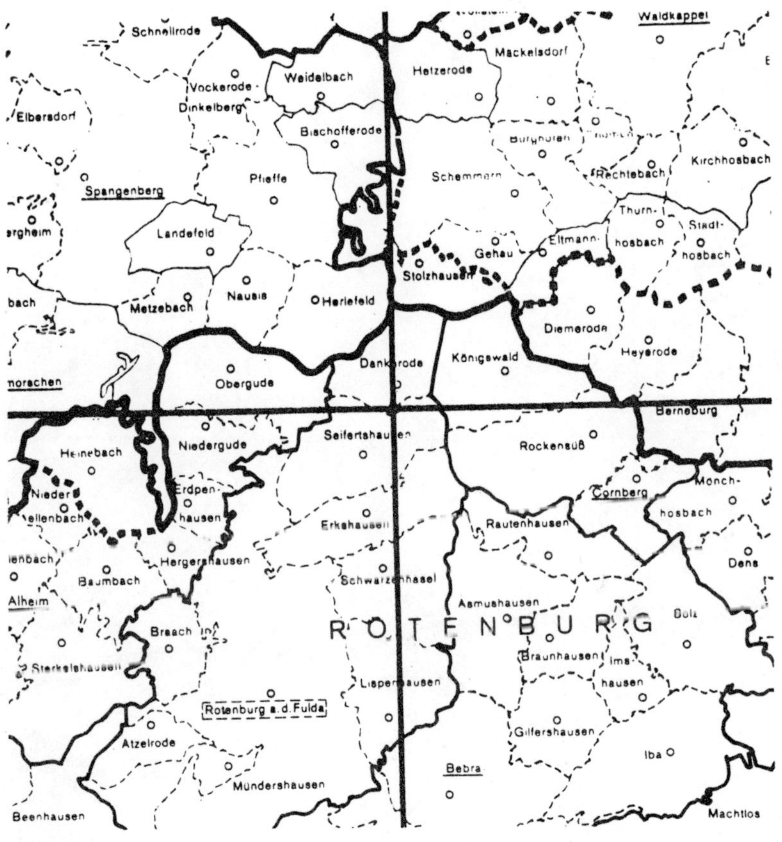

Rotenburg, State of Hessen, Germany
Showing the village boundaries of Dankerode-an-der-Fulda and Erkehausen, home of my Werning, Brehon, and Ort ancestors.

CHAPTER THREE

Preparations for the trip to Germany

What to expect once you are there

If your ancestors immigrated more than one hundred years ago, there will probably not be anyone left in the German "hometown" who knew your emigrant relatives. However, if you think there is a chance that friends, descendants of friends, or living relatives in your ancestors' native village in Germany may remember your emigrant family members, write to the parson of the village church and inquire to verify that such persons exist and request procedures for contacting them. The village church is probably the link to experiencing firsthand the same place where your ancestor worshiped, a way to touching forebearers lives in the 20th century. You may even find as I did at Battenhausen the building preserved almost exactly as it was during your ancestor's lifetime. If there is not a church in the village, write to the Burgermeister (Mayor), c/o City Hall of the closest city and request information about your family for verification purposes. Specific questions get specific answers - ask if your ancestor lived in the village. Are there any living relatives in the village today? Write in either the German or English language and give the full name of your ancestor, the name of the village, and the date of your ancestor's departure from the village, enclosing a self-addressed envelope using the appropriate number of International Reply Coupons (available at all U.S. Post Offices). Air-mail letters are more convenient and faster than surface mail, which takes six weeks or longer to cross the ocean.

For research into an ethnic family a command of the Old World language is indispensable. There are definite limits to what you can accomplish without it. If you do not have a reading knowledge of the language necessary for research in Germany, do not be discouraged. Ask someone who reads and writes German to help you write the letter to make the necessary inquiries to confirm that you have located the village of your immigrant ancestors. If you are not acquainted with anyone of German descent, inquire at your local library or closest university campus language department for assistance in locating such a person. It is, of course, helpful if you can speak or understand the German language when you travel to the Old World. The adult population of most German villages still speak only the German language. An immediate communication barrier is encountered if neither speaker can understand the other.

My limited understanding of and ability to speak German has been accomplished under great difficulty. First, I had to overcome the idea of having been forbidden to learn German despite growing up in a bilingual home and extended bilingual family. Secondly, though I studied one year of academic German in my freshman year in college, it was thirty-five years later that I finally visited my ancestral village for the first time. As a result, I lost many of the German language skills I had learned at a younger age. It was then I found the German language is very perplexing. A highly inflected language, German has three genders, four cases and a strong and weak declension of qualifying adjectives. There are so many grammar rules and so many exceptions to the rules that every time I thought I had mastered a "case" (nominative, dative, accusative, genetic), an insignificant preposition popped up in the sentence. Then I discovered there were more exceptions to the rule than instances of it. The German language has not only a poetic and a philosophical vocabulary, but a scientific and technical terminology as well.

The one thing I liked about German is that all the nouns begin with a capital letter. That makes it easy to identify nouns and facilitates translation. But every noun has a gender and it seems there is no sense or system; therefore, gender has to be memorized. For example, in German a young maiden is neuter (has no sex), but a turnip is female. A tree is male but its buds are female and its leaves are neuter. Dogs are male, cats (including tomcats) are female. Even after learning the sex of a great number of nouns, I still find it difficult to think in terms of "he or she, him or her" and also to know when to refer to "it" to be neuter.

There are ten parts of speech in German and many sentences contain all ten - not in regular order, but mixed. Sentences are often built of compounded new words not found in any dictionary. One must look at the end of the sentence where you locate the verb and find out for the first time what the action of the sentence is. Some German words are so long they really are what Mark Twain called alphabetical processions.

You may discover as I have that German songs are enjoyable because they repeat the same words over and over; for example:

"Du, Du liegst mir im Herzen,
Du, Du liegst mir im Sinn;
Du, Du machst mir viel Schmerzen,
weisst nicht wie gut ich Dir bin;
Ja, ja, ja, ja weisst nicht wie gut ich Dir bin."

Instead of becoming frustrated with the German language, it is best to adopt the humor of Mark Twain who wrote in his essay, "The Awful German Language", suggestions for reforming the German language by leaving out the Dative case, moving verbs further up front in sentences, adding some strong English words to swear with, reorganizing the sexes, and doing away with long compounded words. See *The Complete Humorous Sketches and Tales of Mark Twain* edited by Charles Neider, Hanover House, Garden City, N. Y. 1961.

Planning genealogical research in German village(s)

First contact with your ancestors' Old World village will no doubt be by correspondence. The first contact for information should be for verification of your family records in the Old World indicating that you have found the correct village through your research in the United States. This first request to verify your research must be simply stated and may be written in either the German or English language. Enclose a self-addressed envelope and International Reply Coupons for return postage to facilitate a prompt reply.

Tracing one's ancestors in Germany presents some major problems when it comes to locating a village on a map of the country. The many wars and revolutions in continental Europe, besides economic and natural disasters, and religious and political turmoil have changed the map of Germany. The Thirty Years War in Europe (1618-1648) brought untold destruction to German people and erased much of the family history in many countries on the continent. Few European people can trace their lineage once research reaches the Thirty Years War period of history.

Every researcher of German ancestors is faced with the problems caused by boundary changes. Changes occured following the break-up of the Ottoman Empire between 1830 and 1913 and the Austro-Hungarian Empire in 1918-1919; in 1946, East Germany, or the Deutsche Demokratische Republik (D.D.R.), and West Germany or German Demokratische (G.D.R.) were formed.

The greatest difficulty in locating villages in either East Germany or West Germany is finding a Deutsche Landerkarte (German landmap) with a scale of 1:250,000. It is possible to find German maps of other scales which have numerous cities and towns, but do not include all village locations or the German spelling of names passed down from generation to generation. Much time can be wasted hunting for a specific village that is impossible to find on a map of a the wrong scale. Map symbols indicate which villages have churches. I first wrote to the village of Löhlbach where a church was located to inquire about records for Krug, Paar, Happel, and Möller families. Correspondence led me to research Michel family records at the church in Geismar as indicated by map symbols.

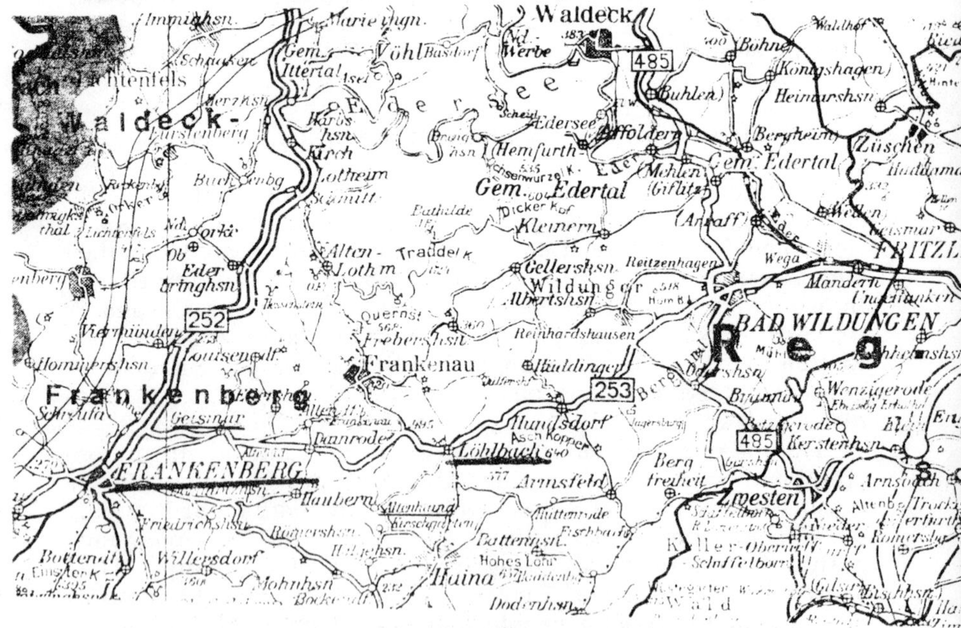

1:250,000 Scale Map
Showing Lohlbach, Battenhausen, and Geismar
Symbol + identifies church; Altenheina has no church

Often times replies to village inquiries are written in German; you may need an interpreter to assist in reading the response. My initial correspondence in English, with the Pfarrer (minister) of the Lohlbach church was never answered because the Pfarrer did not know English and was close to retirement. Several years later I again inquired in English when I learned that there was a new English speaking Pfarrer in the Löhlbach parish. Correspondence followed with a request for an appointment of a convenient time when I could visit in the village and work on genealogy research. I also then requested information about village life of the time my ancestors lived in Lohlbach as well as information about historic costumes of the period.

My next correspondence was in the German language following the Löhlbach minister's suggestion to write in German because Löhlbachers are not bilingual and cannot read English. He also suggested that the place to reside while in the village was at a hotel next door to the church and parsonage where I would be doing my genealogy research. A sketch of the hotel, parsonage where the records were kept and the church helped orient me to the village of my ancestors. I wrote in German to the owner of the Löhlbacher Hof (Lölhbach Hotel) requesting reservations. The following are sample letters:

Date

Sehr geehrte Herr Landau:

Ich plan am 19 Juli nach Deutschland zu fliegen und möchte in Löhlbacher Hof übernachten, ungefähr 3 Nächte. Ich möchte ein Doppelzimmer mit Bad und ein Enzelimmer mit Bad reservieren.

Meine Krug - Happel Familie wohnte in Löhlbach in 18 Jahrhundert und sind nach in 1865 Amerika ausgewandert.

Ich sehr einem Besuch entgegen.

Herzliche Grusse

Honorable Landau family:

I plan to fly to Germany July 22 and would like to stay at the Löhlbacher Hotel for approximately three nights. I wish to make reservations for a double room with bath and a single room with bath.

My Krug - Happel family lived in Löhlbach in the 1800's and emigrated to America in 1865.

I very much look forward to my visit.

Heartfelt (cordial) greetings!

In response to my first request for reservations, the Landau family replied in German (translated to English):

Honorable Mrs. Palen:

I wanted to translate this letter in the language of your country but I'm sure this is also possible for you in your home.

And now about your coming to your old home. The home of your ancestors. I'm sure much has changed during all these years.

It is possible to reserve from 19 July to 22 July (3 days) a room with breakfast. I'm sure you want a room with bath and toilet?

If you want to come later and stay longer, it would also be possible. By now you still don't know exactly when you want to come. Please give me another notice.

Hoping everything will be alright with you, I wish for you all the happiness and fun and success for your trip.
Heartfelt/cordial greetings!

A second letter was required to confirm plans as follows:

Date

Sehr geehrte Herr Landau!

Danke sehr für Ihren lieben Brief, der mir mitteilte dass sie mir ein Doppel-und Einzelzimmer vom 19 ten bis aum 22 ten Juli (3 Tage) mit Früstuck reservieren kömnen.

Wenn ich früher kommen und lönger bleiben will ist es auch möglich.

Ich hoffe, dass alles in ordnung vor sich geht und ich wünsche Ihren viel Freude und spass für Ihre Reise.

Herzliche Grusse!

Honorable Mr. Landau!

Thank you for your dear letter, which informed me that you can reserve for me a double and a single room from 19 to 22 July for three days, including breakfast.

If I want to come earlier and stay longer it will also be possible.

I hope everything will work out as I want it to and I will have fun on the trip.

Heartfelt (cordial) greetings!

Parsonage on Right Front Where Records Are Stored for the Greater Löhlbach Parish Which Consists of Three Congregations. Hotel (Löhlbacher Hof), on upper far right, showa proxomity to church and record storage.

Traveling In East Germany And West Germany

Planning travel to West Germany: Begin preparing for your first visit to Germany as soon as you receive the first favorable response from inquiry about your emigrant ancestor(s).

Transcontinental flights and international tourism today give Americans of German ancestry ease of travel to both East Germany and West Germany to trace their family roots through first-hand observation and person-to-person contact. This makes it possible to gain an increased appreciation of Old World history, traditions, architecture, and landscapes.

What to pack for your Old World Visit: Germany's latitude is 46 degrees (South Germany) to 54 degrees (North Germany) 7 - 15 degrees longitude East of Greenwich. Salem, Oregon, is located on the 45 degree parallel; therefore, Germany is located approximately between Salem, Oregon, and the Canadian border. Western Germany climate is exposed to the influence of the sea and the moist and mild climate of a maritime region. The rainfall, moist and mild climate in Central Germany around Lohlbach encourages the excellent stands of Douglas Fir and the lush vegetation, ferns and undergrowth of the Black Forest floor identical to that found in the Pacific Northwest.

What you take with you depends upon the time of the year you go to Germany. The following list is adequate for spring, summer, and autumn travel. If you are departing in winter, be sure to add a warm coat, gloves, and other warm clothing needed for a colder climate. The best way to travel is to layer clothing that you wear. A blouse/shirt covered by a vest/sweater, covered by a blazer/suit jacket that can be topped by a coat is the best plan. If the weather is hotter or colder, then you can peel off a layer or add a layer for personal comfort. It takes the guessing out of your packing.

Choose a basic color such as navy blue, black, or brown and coordinate all garments and accessories you pack with that color. Then you will have an interchangeable, flexible wardrobe that can be worn many days without becoming monotonous.

A list that will be helpful when packing: one sweater, two dresses/suits, one blazer, one pajamas/robe/slippers, three skirts/pants, three to five blouses/shirts, one swim suit/cap/plastic bag for storage, three to five changes of underwear, two pairs of shoes (comfortable walking shoes and dress shoes), three to five pair of stockings.

A folding umbrella, a light plastic folding raincoat, and a headscarf are essentials to be tucked into your flight bag. A tape recorder, extra tapes and batteries, camera and film are also valuable items to have in your flight bag at all times.

Other items to pack: A file of genealogical records and letter of arrangements made for accommodations, as well as addresses in Germany needed in travel and research. The records you pack depend upon the progress made in searching for your immigrant ancestor(s). Be sure to pack a pedigree chart showing your relationship to your ancestors in Germany since it will be helpful in explaining genealogical research plans to those who may be enlisted to assist with handling your project in your native village. Pack a supply of search sheets, adequate for your planned genealogy goals.

Read completely through your genealogical information before departure day and note particular items of special interest. If you generate a long list of work to be done in your genealogy review, you may find it necessary to set priorities for use of your time in Germany before you travel. Due to the cost of a journey to your native village in Europe and the time taken up by sightseeing, the research part of your trip will necessarily be limited.

Plan your research goals according to the aims of your family history project. Write in advance of your journey for an appointment where you plan to begin your work. Remember to take a file of correspondence and responses received to assist in contact with people and pronounciation of names.

Here's a check-off list of items that should not be forgotten: suitcase key, passport, flight tickets, travelers checks, credit cards, maps, flashlight, electric converter, two pair of eyeglasses, sunglasses, manicure set, sewing kit, pencils with erasers and pens, diary/glue/scissors, address book, washcloth/large bar of soap, and copies of the prescription of any drugs you are taking.

Planning travel to East Germany: The decision whether or not to travel in East Germany should be made before you leave the United States. Application must be made for a visa to travel into East Germany and it takes time to process the visa papers. There is usually no problem about issuing a visa to passengers in a group tour planning to travel together in East Germany. Daily permit fees in East Germany are collected by hotels engaged in tour itinerary. An individual planning to travel alone to East Germany must pay $15.00 a day U.S. money permit fee in addition to visa application and issuance fee paid in the U.S. before departure. The $15.00 per day permit fee is collected and stamped into passport at time of travel at the entry/exit gate in East Germany.

Visiting behind the Iron Curtain is an experience that is interesting to Americans and proved to be the part of my Germany travels that helped me fit the total picture of the life of my ancestors together. They lived in the Old Country known as Prussia. It was in East Germany that I could see the work ethic so important to my family in America, a compulsory style of living still being lived today as the most important value of East German people. I could then understand the strong feelings passed on to me in my learning to do farm chores from an age so young I cannot remember when I did not work on the farm. At the same time I learned to sing Bach Chorales (Johann Sebastian Bach). I learned to read music at the same time as I learned to read and write the English language at the age of five years. Lutherland is so close in proximity to the villages of my ancestors when a dividing border did not exist that the government of the Duke of Saxony and the cities of Dresden and Weimar where Bach, Geothe, Schiller, Luther, Liszt and Wagner lived in East Germany were the important influences at the time of my ancestor's lives in Europe.

We were unable to learn much about East Germany in advance of travel there, except that we would need to be careful about drinking water and that hotels would provide us with bottled water for tooth brushing. We were prohibited from taking into East Germany any newspapers, periodicals, calendars, almanacs, yearbooks, books or literature of any kind the contents of which would be contrary to the interests of the Socialist state. We could not take stamps from any country, collector's coins, weapons, ammunition, television sets or parts to repair televisions, records, tape recordings or toys that had a military character. All drugs were prohibited. Any need for a prescription must be filled before entering the country and taken in at time of entry. No textile items were allowed as presents except textiles and shoes that had been worn and cleaned.

We learned in advance that we would cross the border from West Germany into East Germany near Bad Hersfeld, at Wartha Gate. We would make a customs declaration including an inventory of all money, and fill out a visa form at the border as well as at each East Germany hotel. Once in the country we learned that we should always speak of the D.D.R. or G.D.R. rather than use the words "East Germany." The importance of correct name usage cannot be emphasized too much. The words "East Germany" offend.

In the D.D.R. the fields of grain are large expanses as far as the eye can see to the horizon, the result of collectivization of farms which are state owned and operated. They reminded me of the midwestern grainbelt, the Great Plains in the United States where my German family ancestors settled when they immigrated to the New World.

The D.D.R. has many ancient institutions of learning such as the University of Leipzig established in 1409. Leipzig and the River Elba is also the D.D.R.'s foremost musical city and is the one-time capital of the State of Saxony and present capital of the D.D.R. or G.D.R. We applied for visas to travel in East Germany during the 300th anniversary year of Johann

Sebastian Bach's birthyear and also during the second year of the the two-year celebration of the 500th anniversary of the birthyear of Martin Luther. We read in advance of our travels about the restoration that was underway in the cities we planned to visit for both of the anniversary celebrations. It prepared us to understand what the G.D.R. or D.D.R. guide pointed out as the restored area of the cities we visited.

We could not realize until we visited Dresden, known for its churches and castles, what a city bombed in World War II would look like with the war damage still standing as evidence after forty years of peace. We were awestruck by the ruins called "a heap of shards" remaining after the terrible bombardment of 14 February 1945 which devastated Dresden. The city was undefended and 135,000 people were killed. Only the Zwinger, the baroque palace erected in the 18th Century and later converted into a museum, was restored as a testimonial of the past glories of Dresden.

The D.D.R. government provided our guide, excellent hotels and outstanding food including all meals during our stay.

What To Expect In Germany

Transportation to your ancestral village(s) in Germany: You cannot make travel arrangements of any kind until you find the exact location of the village(s) of your ancestors in West Germany or East Germany. Once you have found the places on the map, you are ready to select the major European airport nearest your village. You can then make flight reservations with an airline, or ask a travel agent to book your flight. The cost is the same whether you book your own flight or have a travel agent do it for you.

If you are fortunate enough to find your village located near a major city you may be able to travel from the airport to the village by train. Depending upon the location of the village you are seeking, you may need to drive by car from the airport to the village(s). The savings in time not spent in trains and buses, waiting for connections, can be put to use researching your genealogy.

Renting a car: To rent a car, telephone any American travel agent before you go to Europe and schedule a rental car. In order to make necessary arrangements, you must know how long you wish the car, and the size of the car you prefer. There are car rental agencies at the airports in Europe, but if you wait to rent a car until you get there and the car you rent needs repair during your travels in Europe, you must foot the bill and be reimbursed when you turn the car back in. If you make arrangements in the United States for an American rental car, you simply pick it up at the car rental desk located in the airport when you arrive in Europe. Then, if it needs repairs, the American car rental company will replace it immediately and you will not have to pay for the repairs. This is the most helpful arrangment in managing the amount of money to take along to Europe.

If you plan to make arrangements to rent a car after arrival in Europe it will be necessary to apply for an International Driver's License.

If you make arrangements for your rental car in the United States before you leave for Europe, it will be possible to use your current state driver's license in Europe and unnecessary to have an International Driver's License.

Driving in West Germany: Roads are excellent for safe driving throughout West Germany. The autobahn is a freeway like our interstate highway system with multiple lanes and no speed limit. Remember when driving:

Keep to the right lane of the highway. Use left lane only for passing.

There are no speed limits on West German highways or on the autobahn. The only speed limits are in cities.

Use of seat belts is required. Fines are imposed for not using them in West Germany.

All highway signs and markers are written in the German language. If you cannot read German quickly be sure to take along a German translator assigned that responsibility.

Driving in East Germany: We crossed over from West Germany at Wartha (Frankfurt/Main-Eisenach) one of twenty-two road crossing points into East Germany. Foreign cars pay a road toll tax. There are speed limits on all roads including the autobahn (63 m.p.h.). All the roads we traveled were in good repair. Keep to the right lane the same as in West Germany.

Coping with the German language barrier: Many German children are learning English in school today. If you are fortunate you may be able to find a student to help you translate in English when reading German signs or speaking to adults you meet. The beautiful Gothic letters used in the alphabet all over Germany intrigued me, stimulating my desire to want to read the German language wherever possible. Without a doubt, in future years, it will be easier to speak English in Germany when more of the young people have studied English longer and are grown to adulthood.

Food in West Germany: It is easy to find good food and excellent restaurants throughout West Germany. The bakery shops that serve hot drinks and sweets were favorite places to stop for a quick snack or coffee break. A feast to your eyes, the luscious fruit glazed flans, tortes, and decorative pastries are all different from what we are accustomed to seeing in the New World.

Breakfast in Germany is a delightful selection of fruit juice, toast, rolls, slices of several kinds of dark breads, thinly sliced meats, cheeses, and eggs, cereals, jams and jellies. The local cheese served varies according to the area of Germany you are visiting. Spreads for toast and breads include Beirwurst (beerwurst) or Kalbsleberwurst (liver-wurst).

Excellent noon-hour meals are served in hotels in West Germany at a reasonable cost.

Abendessen (Evening Meal) in German family homes is often a selection of rolls and breads, cheeses, sliced meats, jams, tea and coffee, a menu similar to breakfast with the addition of a sweet torte for dessert.

Food in East Germany: Hotel meals are excellent and served in multiple courses. Breakfast included pepper cheese and jagdwurst, cucumber slices, cherry tomatoes/parsley in addition to rolls, bread, eggs, ham & sausage, cereals. Hotel Merkur in Leipzig served smorgasbord buffets for breakfast and the evening dinner including caviar and truffles, steak and many kinds of meat, mohnkuchen (poppy seed filling) decorated desserts and ices, fruits and cakes.

Lunch while touring cities was eaten in restaurants that were convenient and consisted of interesting combinations of familiar foods to westerners and some new vegetables such as boiled red bell peppers cut in strips. Hungarian and Russian dishes were on the menus.

We ate at the famous Auerbachs Keller (since 1525) in Leipzig where Wolfgange Goethe drank wine in 1766 and encountered Dr. Faust and the devil "Mein Leipzig lob ich mir!" ("Leipzig, I praise you!)

Menu: Berlin Beefsalad with Bread, or Mephistofleisch (Mephisto was the main character of Faust - meat) with

French Fries and Vegetable Salad. Local people eat a lot of pork.

Speciality Foods: One of the pleasures of traveling in Germany is tasting some of the specialties of the country. I looked forward to seeing and tasting the local cheeses called landcase and the local sausages called landjager served in every area. In Munich we ate their original white sausage with pickled cabbage and homemade small flour dumplings. The sausage served at Fulda at Hotel Lenz tasted exactly like the sausage recipe my German Great-Grandparents passed down to my generation through the years.

There are specialty beverages also that are refreshing. Berliner Weiss (beer with raspberry juice) was delicious. Bitter Lemon was a refreshing drink in the middle of a warm summer day. The sign: "There is no beer in heaven, therefore, we drink it here" motivates the drinking of light and dark beer. If you do not care for beer, it is customary to order Spezi, a non-alcoholic drink, dark in appearance, served in beer mugs that looks exactly to your friends like you are drinking with them, when in reality you have a non-alcoholic drink of cola and a lemon carbonated mixture. Tasse Espresso is Expresso Coffee.

If you order a hamburger-type sandwich in West Germany, it will be served with a fried egg on top of the meat.

German Currency: The pfenning (pfg.) and Deutsche Mark (DM) are the units of currency in both West Germany and East Germany. It is not difficult to calculate German currency when one remembers that there are one hundred pfenning in a Deutsche Mark. Both East Germany and West Germany have their own paper money and coins which are not interchangeable and cannot be used other than in the country of origin. At the time of our visit, the exchange rate for U.S. currency was exactly the same in both West Germany and East Germany.

Travelers Checks are the best way to carry money with you when you travel abroad. If you carry American Express checks the best exchange rate is made at the American Express offices in Europe. Banks also give a better exchange rate than hotels or businesses that accept travelers checks.

BERLIN
W
E
EAST GERMANY
KASSEL
Geismar
Battenhausen
Attenhain
Dankerode
on
the Fulda
Wartha Gate
Eisenach
Erfurt
Weimar
LEIPZIG
DRESDEN
Airport
Erkshausen
FRANKFURT
WEST GERMANY
MUNICH

CHAPTER FOUR

Research To Do In Germany

Thousands of villages, castles, and many churches which housed records of births, deaths, and marriages were destroyed during the wars initiated by the Protestant Reformation. As a result, it is very difficult even for Europeans to trace their ancestry before this time (1650).

Civil registration began in all areas of the former German Empire in 1876. Church registers began in Saxony soon after 1550, and in some of the other parts of Germany as late as the Seventeenth or even Eighteenth Century. Civil registers prior to 1876 are aften kept in the town hall and sometimes in archives of the district. Civil registers since 1876 are kept in the office of civil registers (Standesamt). Some church and civil registers of the areas under Soviet and Polish rule since World War II are kept in West Berlin. In some communities west of the Rhine River the church archives may sometimes be found in the mayor's office.

Since the immigration of my German ancestors occured before 1875, the primary source of genealogy for my family was in the church records that began following the Reformation. They were residents of Prussia at that time. Early church registers in most Protestant communities were under ordinances decreed by the prince ruling the country. In Saxony an advanced administrative system already existed in the mid-Sixteenth Century. In Hessen-Nassau where my German ancestors lived, the Lutherans and Calvinists were united in 1818 and their combined church registers are called "Evangelical". Approximately sixty-one percent of the present-day population in the State of Hessen is Protestant. Due to many territorial and geographical changes in Hessen history there is no one central archive to search for records. At one time in history the Hessen territory was named Hessen-Nassau as the name appeared on the American family name appeared on the American family birth records of my Happel-Werning relatives. (See research addresses in Bibliography.) Kassel was the seat of government of the Landgrave (Count or Prince) of Hesse-Kassel and well-known as the place where the Landgrave employed librarians known as "Brothers Grimm". (They collected and published Hessian folktales in 1812 and 1815 which became known as "Grimm's Fairytales"). The town hall at Kassel was bombed during World War II and many civil records destroyed.

Many of the castles in Germany which housed state archives suffered losses in World War II. In East Germany many of these archives entered the state archives in Saxony in 1946, and are now known as the "Schönburg archives".

Usually primary sources can be found in West Germany at either the city hall or parish register. A thorough search to find records of an area must be made if a record cannot be located where it was made; it may still exist in an archive of the state (Staatarchiv) national or provincial, city, district, village or family archive.

PRIMARY SOURCES

Birth, marriage and death certificates - search civil and parish registers first. Birth dates may be found in marriage and death records. If records do not exist it is possible to verify calculated dates through confirmation records, Guild records, census records, police registration required at time of moving, court records, probate records or newspapers. Clues to vital record information may also be found in family registers, grave registers, church receipt books, funeral sermons, city chronicles and land records. In East Germany search for civil registration at the County Council Offices.

Church Records - often stored at the parsonage or at parish storage in nearby villages. In villages such as Löhlbach (dating from 800 A.D.) parish records begin soon after the Reformation. Grave registers and church receipt books may be availabe in addition to Baptism, Confirmation, Marriage, Burial and Family Registers.

School Records - located at the particular school of interest. Useful to verify full names and parent's signatures.

Legal Contracts - search at city hall and land archives to verify land ownership, signatures of owners.

Kirburg am 17. Dezember 1882.

Vor dem unterzeichneten Standesbeamten erschien heute, der

Persönlichkeit nach __________ bekannt,

der Landmann Friedrich Weyand

wohnhaft zu Neunkhausen

evangelischer Religion, und zeigte an, daß von der

Emilie Weyand geborene Pfeiffer

seiner Ehefrau

evangelischer Religion,

wohnhaft bei ihm

zu Neunkhausen in seiner Wohnung

am sechzehnten Dezember des Jahres

tausend acht hundert achtzig und zwei Vormittags

um drei Uhr ein Kind weiblichen

Geschlechts geboren worden sei, welches die Vornamen

Emma

erhalten habe

Vorgelesen, genehmigt und unterschrieben

Friedrich Weyand.

Der Standesbeamte.

H. Maage.

A City Hall Birth Registration In West Germany

Tax Bills - may be found in city or county archives. Verifies location, names of owners.

Mortgages - search county archives to verify names, evidence of residency and location.

Business Licenses - may be found in city archives to verify occupation, location, names of partnership.

Income Tax Forms - search in city archives or district archives to verify legal names and addresses.

Wills - find in either District Court House or State archives (Provincial). In East Germany search at the Office of States Notary in county. Verifies legal names of children and closest family members.

Letters and Diaries - search city libraries, museums, city hall and may be found in homes of civil authorities. Source of names of family members, relatives, events, and dates.

Census Records - copies of federal government census in West Germany are located in municipal archives or the District Registry Office in each city or district. In East Germany census results are destroyed after counting is completed. Verifies names of family members and years of residency.

Military Records - search State Archives for verification of names, birth date and place, names of parents.

Land Deeds - may be found in Provincial Archives (State and Landarchives). Sometimes found in city archives. Verifies residency and legal names.

Court Records - may be found in Provincial Archives (State and Landarchives). Sometimes found in city archives. Verifies legal names and addresses.

SECONDARY SOURCES

Cemetery Inscriptions - in many parts of Germany it will be impossible to read cemetery inscriptions because cemetery plots are not maintained after 30 years and are resold. If another family member buys the cemetery plot at the end of 30 years, it sometimes remains in the same family for 60 years or more. Therefore, it is impossible to find burial sites of ancestors of the 17th, 18th, 19th, and even 20th centuries.

Obituaries - found in city libraries, parish archives, family libraries. Valuable sources of names of village of residency and birth.

Bible Records - search for in family archives for family full names, dates of birth, baptism, confirmation, marriage, death and burials.

Newspaper Clippings - city libraries, provincial archives (State and Landarchives) and family libraries may be source for births, marriages, death notices and other family events of a lifetime.

Interpreting Handwriting - Genealogy Research: I had been warned that it would not be easy to read German records. To prepare for the experience, I had my father write a German alphabet. Both had been schooled in the German language. They explained the difficulty in reading and writing German was the many precise slants to the letters and strokes in vertical style in German handwriting which I had often heard referred to as "chicken scratching." There are several references useful in improving skills in reading German (Storrer and Jensen 1977 and Walker 1977). The three authors collaborated in using the same examples in their books to reinforce learning German language skills (See Bibliography).

The Latin alphabet, both upper-case and lower-case letters, are the same as in English and are included here for comparison with the German alphabet and the Gothic print used in Germany.

The German handwriting style of earlier centuries greatly slowed my progress as it was very difficult to read. Interpreting it challenges one to study ancient handwriting known as paleography. Note examples of German script showing the challenge facing the genealogist researching in person in German village records.

German Handwriting

In East Germany all church registers were destroyed in the Seven Years' War of the 1760,'s and again in the bombing of World War II. Old registers of deeds, mortgages and Burgher Rolls registering citizenship are the primary sources of information in such instances. Citizenship applications give birth or baptism certificates with the names and the profession of parents and grandparents.

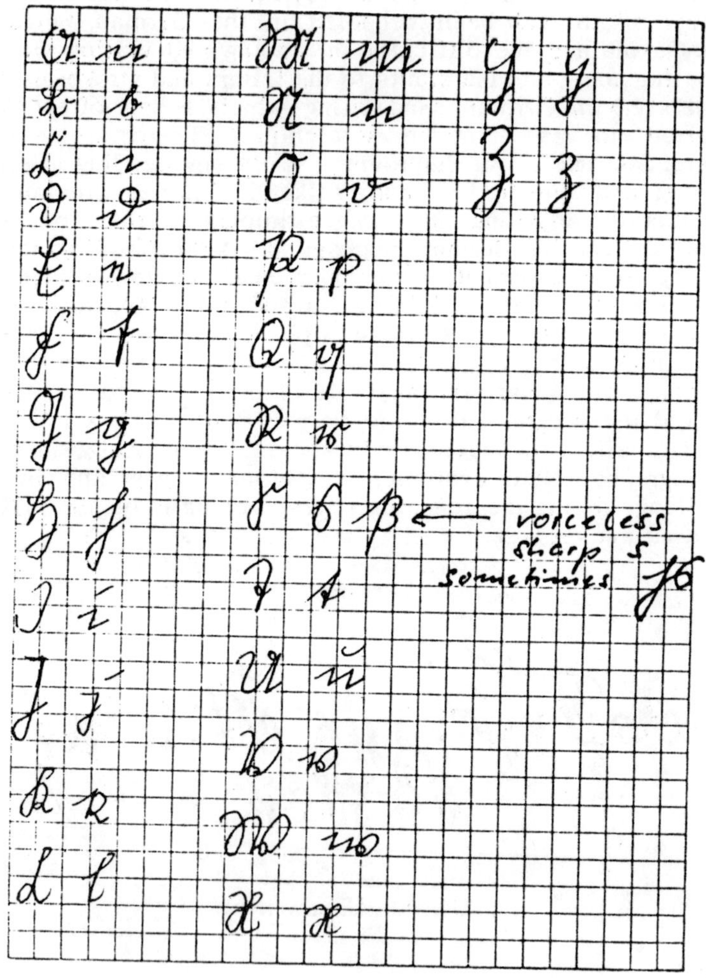

German Alphabet

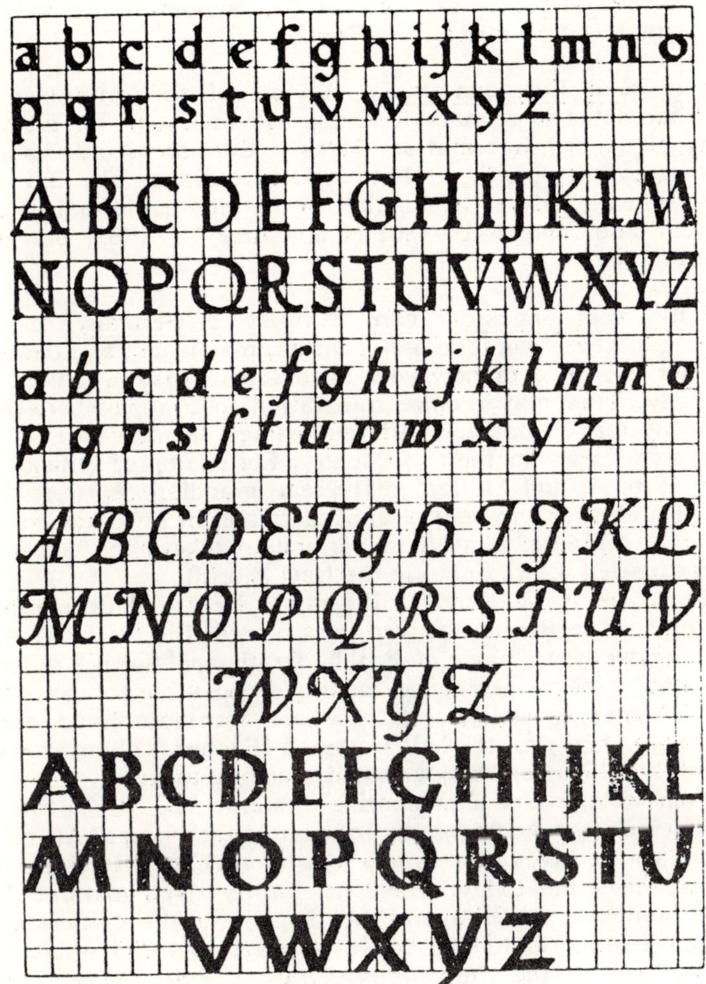

Latin Alphabet

Most of the church registers in West Germany are kept in the archives of the parish. However, in Dankerode-an-Der-Fulda the church records, (Werning family records) which date from 1762, are from a congregation and building that dates back to 1691 and they are kept at Schwarzenhasel, a village approximately four miles from Dankerode.

How to read European dates: Review of the difference in recording dates in records in Europe is necessary to prevent faulty genealogy information. Dates in German records have a form in reverse of U.S. vital statistic recordings. The day always appears before the number of the month and that before the year date. Thus 6-10-1862 is not June 10, 1862, but October 6, 1862.

How did your ancestors earn a living in Germany? In the process of searching records for births, marriages, and deaths, look for evidence of how your ancestors earned a living in Germany. This may require translation in Europe where cultural differences decreed different names for occupations in earlier centuries in the Old Country. For example, I found my Krug, Happel, and Moller great-great grandfathers were recorded as either a maurer or an Achermann in Lohlbach or Altenhaina. A maurer is a bricklayer and an ackermann is a farm worker (called a hired man in the New World).

Houses in West German villages are identified by number. The number of the house lived in is recorded in the baptismal record under item "place of birth". Death and funeral records also list place of residence making it possible to locate the actual homes in villages today where ancestors lived many years ago. Many of the half timbered (Fachwerk) houses built in 18th and 19th centuries are still standing today.

Each village has a numbering system. The #1 house in Lohlbach is the home of the forester of the village. All other numbers were given many years ago in order at that time and remain the same today. The Krug family lived in three different homes in the village of Lohlbach over the centuries of record keeping including house #3, #70 and #33 where the family lived at the time of immigration. I visited all three houses.

CHAPTER FIVE

Writing Family History

You need not wait until every last detail about your family has been discovered before you turn attention to sharing the information you have already researched. Bridging the years of family history - from the time of immigration to contemporary years - requires summarizing your family research.

In the process of writing family history, you may discover clues to why owning property meant so much to your family, or why your family was especially interested in fruit orchards or gardening. The answer may exist thousands of miles away in the Old World. You may find your family originally was fleeing political oppression, financial hard times or hunger due to crop failure. The simple, strong desire to create a better life for themselves and their families caused thousands of German people to look to the New World for their future.

The information collected about forefathers and their interests can add to knowledge about your family and be a rewarding, adventuresome experience.

Your family history is unique and your ancestral heritage is a part of the events of the first two hundred years of a New World nation. The most clannish of immigrant families in America sooner or later mingled with neighbors to assimilate New World language and increase social opportunities leading to marriage for the youngest generation.

To write a family history, you need to make several decisions:

1. What would you like your finished family history to look like? Will it include photos? Will it be narrative style with biographical stories? How much history will you weave into your family story? Will you use the method of the family pedigree as a framework for writing about your family? How

much detail will you include in reproduction of important documents of relatives lives?

Before you make final decisions, you will want to consider the costs involved in producing your family history. Photos and reproductions of documents add considerably to the cost of the book. Before deciding about your family history, what should be included and what should be left out, keep in mind the fact that another generation will look at it from a different viewpoint. A later generation might appreciate details which to you might seem irrelevant in the total history.

Be sure to write in a positive vein, including the best that can be said about your family. Include quotations from persons, word-for-word, whenever possible. Let the personalities add to the presentation of your family history. The details of lives will be of much interest to descendants in years to come. Reader interest is increased if writing is in the first person, using the pronouns "I" and "we" rather than writing in the passive and quoting in the third person as an observer.

If unfavorable data is found, include it and carefully document the source and date the information was researched. Future research may clear up the circumstances surrounding the data and explain it completely for all future generations. An example is my finding in the Lölhbach Kirche (church) records that both my Krug and Happel forefathers in Europe married into the same Moller family, more than one generation, going back as far as the 1700's. Since my Krug and Happel grandparents married in the New World, it means there are multiple intermarriages in their family lineage. Future research is needed to clarify specifically all the relationships.

2. How will the materials be organized? The organization of the material often takes longer than the actual writing of the family history. It takes much time to identify each family photograph and write its story. If help is needed about how to prepare photos, consult with the printer before you go too far into the project. Reproduced documents add to reader interest also. Keep in mind the costs involved in adding details to your family history. It is common to find estimated costs fall short of the actual cost of a finished project. Allow for this probability as you progress in writing your family history.

3. What methods will you use? The size of the history, the size of the type used in printing, the quality of paper used, and how the history is bound will all be considerations for the final cost and determine the method of finishing your family history. In determining the number of copies to be printed, al-

low extras for presentation to local libraries in towns where the family resided.

A systems approach is useful in thinking about family genealogical research:

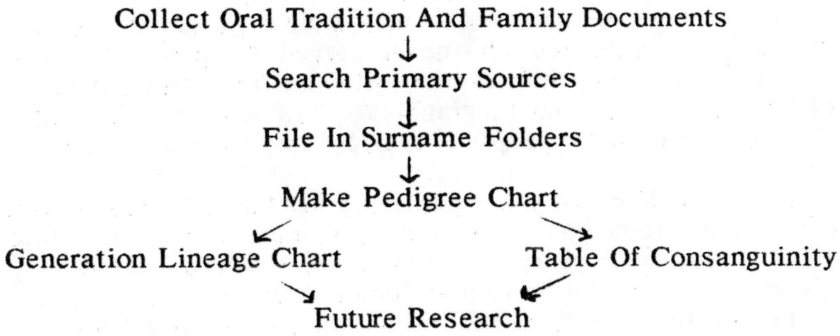

Collect Oral Tradition And Family Documents
↓
Search Primary Sources
↓
File In Surname Folders
↓
Make Pedigree Chart
↙ ↘
Generation Lineage Chart | Table Of Consanguinity
↘ ↙
Future Research

It is helpful to take the time to study family kinship. Throughout the world kinship can provide a study of the various differences in the face of a culture. It is very interesting to trace kinship descent bilaterally through both parents. Draw out a horizontal generation chart which shows the lineage since immigration in the U.S.A. to the present generation. Simply take the name of the immigrant ancestor and write it at the top of a page of legal-size paper along with the year of birth and the names of any brothers or sisters research has revealed. Skip a space and write the names and birth dates of all the children in the next generation on a horizontal line. Continue to write the names and birth dates of each generation on separate lines to include the present generation. Now underline the names and draw an arrow from your direct ancestor to the name of the next generation direct ancestor from whom you are descended. When finished you will have a page which will show you at a glance the size of each generation from whom you are directly descended and the person that is your direct ancestor. It gives a perspective on other branches of the family in a simple and easy system to understand.

When you have completed a generation lineage chart it is very valuable to draw out kinship relationship on a Table of Consanguinity. This is a more time consuming task, but well worth the effort to clarify exactly your first, second, and third cousins; in addition to showing you who your cousins removed are in each generation of the family. It assists the realization that kinship and descent relationships are the basis for behavior in families. In all societies kinship expectations determine the obligations and duties of the family members. Once you have examined the form of the consanguinity chart it is easy to determine the relationships of direct family lines by taking the time to write out the names of the people in each square that applies to the correct relationship.

Most people researching family genealogy are descended from ordinary families who never served the public nor attained prominence through the ministry or other positions where it is easy to find biographical sketches, memoirs, etc. To research ordinary people it is necessary to go to public archives.

Once you have finished gathering all the information you can locate from home and family sources and from public sources, and have worked out a method for writing your family history, the next step is to plan future research.

Perseverance is required to search your family back one hundred or more years. If your ancestors were among the enormous number of immigrants who came into the United States in the middle 1800's, you may discover you can trace them through federal census records in which individuals in the last half of the nineteenth century were asked to identify their parent's state or country of birth. This will make it possible for you to continue your search back into more years of family history. It is a challenge to see how far you can trace your family in genealogy research.

If you feel you have reached a stopping point in your genealogy research and need the help of a professional genealogist to assist with future work, contact the Board of Certification of Genealogists, 1307 New Hampshire Avenue, N.W., Washington, D.C., for a listing of certified genealogists in your area. Genealogists are also available through the Genealogical Society, 50 E. North Temple Street, Salt Lake City, Utah 84150.

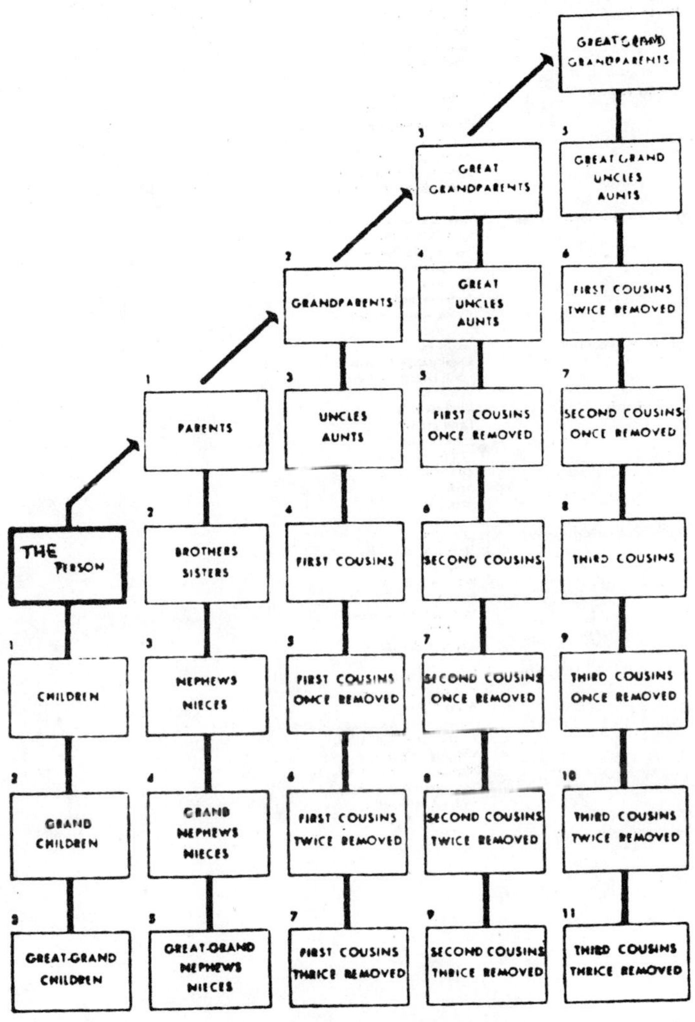

Table Of Consanguinity

RESEARCH CHECK LIST

Name:
Relationship:
Inclusive dates:
Parents:

Location of sources:	*Type*	*Date*	*Location of notes:*
Home	Family Bible		
	Family letters		
	Interviews		
	Photographs		
County records	Vital records		
	Marriage records		
	Wills, estates, etc.		
	Deeds, etc.		
	Mortgages		
	Other recorders' records		
	Naturalization records		
Town records and libraries	City or county directories		
	Cemetery records/grave. insc.		
	Ms. or pub. histories		
	Newspaper files		
	Tax lists		
	Voter records		
	Public school records		
Church depositories	Archives		
	Local parish records		
	Local church histories		
State records	Vital records		
	Land grants		
	State census		
	Militia records		
	Tax lists		
	Archives		
	Acts, journals		
National records	Censuses		
	Mortality schedules		
	Military records		
	Pension records		
	Passenger lists		
	Immigration records		
	Land records		
	Special records		
Libraries	Indexes, special		
	Printed & ms. genealogies		
	Printed histories		
	Occupational histories		
	Biographical compendia		
	Manuscript histories		
	Obituary collections/indexes		
	Cemetery records/grave. insc.		
	Abstract volumes		
Correspondence			

BIBLIOGRAPHY

American Society of Genealogists, *Genealogical Research: Methods and Sources*, Washington, D.C. 1960–1971.

Arbeitsgeminschaft Ostdeufscher Familienforscher e.V. Herne, Germany (Union of East German Family Researchers), *Genealogical Guide to German Ancestors From East Germany and Eastern Europe*, Verlag Degener and Co. Neustadt/Aisch., West Germany 1984.

Baxter, Agnus. *In Search of Your European Roots. A Complete Guide to Tracing Your Ancestors in Every Country in Europe*. Genealogical Publishing Co., Inc., Baltimore, MD. 1985.

Greenwood, Val D. *The Researcher's Guide to American Genealogy*. Genealogical Publishing Company, Inc., Baltimore, MD. 1978.

Jensen, Larry O. *A Genealogical Handbook of German Research*. P.O. Box 441, Pleasant Grove, Utah. 1978.

Kretschmer, Albert. *Das grosse Buch der Volkstrachten*. Rheingauer Verlagsgesellschaft. Eltville am Rhein 1982

National Archives and Records Service. *Guide to Genealogical Research in the National Archives*. National Archives and Records Service, Washington, D.C. 1985.

Neagles, James C. and Lila Lee. *Locating Your Immigrant Ancestor*. The Everton Publishers, Inc., Logan, Utah. 1975

Smith, Clifford Neal and Anna Piszczan-Czaja. *American Genealogical Resources in German Archives*. Verlag Dokumentation. Publishers, Munchen. 1977.

Smith, Clifford Neal. *Encyclopedia of German-American Genealogical Research.* New York and London, R. R. Bowker Company, 1976.

Storrer, Norman J. and Larry O. Jensen. *A Genealogical and Demographic Handbook of German Handwriting 17th - 19th Centuries.* Vol. I, Pleasant Grove, Utah. 1977.

The Source: A Guidebook of American Genealogy. Edited by Arlene Eakle and Johni Cerny. Ancestry Publishing Company, Salt Lake City, Utah. 1984.

Walker, Ronald D. *A Genealogical Handbook of German Terminology and Grammar.* Sandy, Utah. 1977.

Research Addresses

Municipal Archives: Stadtsarchiv, D/3500 Kassel, West Germany

Hessen-Kassel Archives: Staatsarchiv, Frederickplatz 15, D/3550 Marburg, West Germany

Genealogical Society

Arbeitsgemeinschaft fur Familienforscchung, Emilienstrasse 1, D/3500 Kassel, West Germany

Kurhessen and Waldeck Genealogical Society

Gesellschaft fur Familienkunde (in Kurhessen und Waldeck), Ellingroederstrasse 5, D/6413 Rotenberg/Fulda, West Germany

INDEX